Management Development
Strategies for Action

Management Development
Strategies for Action

Alan Mumford

Second Edition

Institute of Personnel Management

© Institute of Personnel Management, 1989, 1993

First published 1989
Second edition 1993

Phototypeset by
The Eastern Press Ltd (Typesetting Division)
Frome, Somerset
and printed in Great Britain by
SRP Ltd, Exeter, Devon.

British Library Cataloguing in Publication Data
   Mumford, Alan
   Management Development: Strategies for
   Action.—2Rev.ed
   I. Title
   658.3

   ISBN 0–85292–518–2

Contents

Figures

Acknowledgements

The then Manpower Services Commission, now the Training Agency, sponsored the research projects 'Learning to learn for managers' and 'Developing directors – the learning processes'. I am grateful to them for having given me the opportunity to do the research, publish it and use it in other books, especially *Developing top managers*.

I am also grateful to Gower, the publishers of *Developing top managers*, for agreeing that I could use some of the charts and figures from that book here; and to *Personnel Management*, for permission to reprint (in adapted form) the exercise which appears at the end of Chapter 9.

My colleagues at International Management Centres were supportive of the idea that I should write another book, and I am grateful to them, and of course to the Institute of Personnel Management, for suggesting it.

The books makes use of a wide variety of experiences with different employers and a large number of managers. John Laing and, particularly, Don Stradling gave me my first opportunities in management development. My subsequent work has been built on the sound base of this early experience. I was given opportunity, challenge, sensitively conducted review processes – and sent on some good courses. If this book helps others to have similarly good experiences, then part of my early debt to John Laing will be repaid.

Finally, my thanks to Richard Wright for his help in improving the book.

Introduction

The IPM has led the way in continuous learning, and in fulfilling the need to integrate formal and informal development, through its ABCD campaign and its book *Continuous development*. I was delighted to be asked to write this present work since my own ideas relate so clearly to those themes.

It is more than twenty years since the IPM published the first edition of Tom Roberts's *Developing effective managers*. I read it and used it then and have remained impressed with it when I have subsequently revisited it.

The common ground between this book and Tom Roberts's lies largely in the area of what I now call formal management development schemes and processes. The major difference of focus is in the area of informal management development. Two earlier books of mine, *Making experience pay* and *Developing top managers*, gave considerable attention to informal learning. The first was written to challenge the focus on formal management development of most other books on the subject, while the second is a research-based analysis aimed particularly at the top levels of management. These books do not, therefore, cover the formal aspects of management development in enough detail to offer a comprehensive view of the topic which is suitable for managers at all levels. This the present book sets out to do, while sharing with my two earlier books a belief that learning is the central issue; it is not inputs which define the success of management development, but output.

I have attempted to write a book which is innovative without being fanciful; its ideas are not wholly untested. They are based on nearly thirty years of experience in management development, for most of which time I was employed as an in-company management development adviser. My later experience at an innovative business school, International Management Centres, has provided me with the opportunity to carry out research on the learning and development processes of managers and directors.

I believe that the combination of these two different kinds of experience has enabled me to write a better book than I would have written five years ago. Up till then I had had the experience of sitting with the top five executives of my company and helping them make decisions about whether a senior manager should go on a course at the London Business School, and whether another manager should be sent to run a new company in South-East Asia or should be given a new role coordinating marketing in Europe. My research experiences since then enabled me not only to collect different views on the ways in which such problems should be approached in planning formal management development, but to understand better why such decisions are not often made as part of a coolly reflective, long-term planning process.

DEFINITIONS

The terms and processes of 'manager development', 'management development' and 'organization development' merge into one another both in understanding and practice. In this introduction it is only necessary to say that I use management development to describe the total process by which managers learn and grow in effectiveness; I do not regard it merely as the third leg of a tripod (the other two being management education and management training).

THE CHAPTER SEQUENCE

The chapters follow one another in a logical sequence. However, this sequence reflects my own views of where we need to start in order to understand and implement management development processes. Some readers may arrive at the book with different ideas about what is significant and important which may influence where they want to start.

I recommend that everyone starts with Chapter 1. Those who are initially particularly interested in formal management development processes could then choose to read Chapter 2, followed by Chapters 4–8. Readers who are in the first instance more interested in informal processes may prefer to follow Chapter 1 with Chapters 3, 9 and 11.

However, since it is my opinion that we need to draw informal and formal processes together, the book makes most sense if read in the sequence in which it is written.

CATERING FOR DIFFERENCES

One of the major challenges in management development is coping with individual differences: differences in needs, differences in preferred approaches to learning, differences between men and women. I have already tried to show that I intend to practise what I preach in this book by offering suggestions about the different sequences the reader might choose.

Another of the book's themes is that development most frequently occurs as a result of managers actually taking action. Most modern management development advisers would also subscribe to the view that development is something you undertake and achieve for yourself; it is not something 'done to' you. It is therefore appropriate that in many parts of the book I will be suggesting development activities which advisers can test out on themselves; there can after all be no better recommendation when offering these processes to managers!

FURTHER READING

Chapters 12 and 13 provide balance by listing not only additional material on the points made in the book, but also references to views which differ from my own.

Introduction to the Second Edition

The substance of this book, prepared for publication in May 1989, required no major alterations, although references have been updated where appropriate to later editions of books. The main text remains unchanged because the themes and proposals identified in it have not been affected by subsequent events. If anything, there has been a move towards a greater awareness of what needs to be done to make management development effective through work on the job.

Where new material *has* become available, it seemed to me appropriate to cover it in terms of particular issues, and then to offer a few general reflections on recent trends, rather than to include separate references for each chapter. In this second edition, therefore, new material is drawn together in a new Chapter 13. Readers should check after reading each chapter whether any further details appear there.

1 Starting from Where You Are

A PARADOX IN MANAGEMENT DEVELOPMENT

- Managers often say 'I learned to be a manager from experience'
- Managers quite often lack the skills and knowledge necessary to do their jobs fully effectively

It is to fill the gap between these two statements that formal management development processes have been designed – to widen the range of experience, to give specific training in particular skills and to provide knowledge of the context in which the manager operates. The paradox is that managers continue to think of learning and development as being essentially and primarily about the work experiences they have had, whereas personnel and management development advisers think about management development mainly in terms of planned processes of job rotation, succession planning and courses.

A second paradox is that while personnel directors will often talk about formal processes of development to others, their own personal development experiences have often, just like managers', been informal and accidental.

PERSONAL EXPERIENCES OF DEVELOPMENT

You can test how far you believe these paradoxes to be true, first for yourself and then for others. Here is an exercise.

Exercise

1   Look back over your managerial career and identify:
    - your two most significant/important/helpful learning experi-
      ences
    - your two least significant/important/helpful learning experi-
      ences

Or perhaps you would prefer a less specifically focused exercise.

2   Look back at your life and pick out the major events in it which
    have helped to make you the person you are. Assess each event
    by defining:
    - Your feelings about it then/your feelings about it now
    - What do you think you learned from that experience at that
      time?
    - Have you learnt something new or different by looking at it
      now?

When you have completed either or both of these exercises, consider
your response to the paradoxes stated at the beginning of this
section.

3   How far have the best and worst of your experiences been
    planned/formal/structured, as compared with informal experi-
    ences within and around your work?
4   Think about the managerial group with which you have the closest
    connections. How far have they been developed through formal
    processes and how far through informal processes?

You may want some assistance in checking and clarifying your
answers both for yourself and for your colleagues. Figure 1.1 may
jog your memory, especially about some of the formal processes
to which you have been exposed. Figure 1.2 illustrates situations
or people from which you may have learned within and around
the job.
     Here are two examples of replies to this exercise.

> My boss took time in joint problem solving to let me
> reach my own conclusions, coaching me as necessary

Figure 1.1 Methods of Learning Off the Job

Books	Business games
Lectures	Simulations
Programmed learning	T groups
Interactive video	Demonstration and practice
Films	Role plays
Group discussion	Outdoor
Case study	Discovery
In tray	Diagnostic instruments

Figure 1.2 Learning Opportunities

The opportunities identified here are not necessarily separate. You may, for example, think of something first in terms of something happening at a meeting – or you may think of the way in which one of your colleagues achieved success at a meeting.

Situations within the organization	*Processes*
Meetings	Coaching
Task – familiar	Counselling
– unfamiliar	Listening
Task force	Modelling
Customer visit	Problem solving
Visit to plant/office	Observing
Managing a change	Questioning
Social occasions	Reading
Foreign travel	Negotiating
Acquisitions/mergers	Mentoring
Closing something down	Public speaking
	Reviewing/auditing
Situations outside your organization	Clarifying responsibilities
Charity	Walking the floor
Domestic life	Visioning
Industry committee	Strategic planning
Professional meetings	Problem diagnosis
Sports club	Decision making
	Selling
	People
	Boss
	Mentor
	Network contacts
	Peers
	Consultants
	Subordinates

through my thinking processes. Sometimes this led to outcomes which he probably anticipated. He was able to think laterally and find answers to questions which sometimes seemed impossible to solve. In those situations he coached me in the techniques he favoured.

This was from a man in his mid-20s.

The next example is from a senior director.

I did an MBA after five years' work experience. It was my initiative to go on it. I have found the jobs I have done, and the movement between different functions, very interesting. What I did not understand was how things really worked, who pulled things together, and what it was all about in terms of principle rather than detail. I wanted to know how things fitted together into a conceptual framework. The MBA gave me that framework, a base for continued intellectual stimulus, and an assurance that problems were actually analysable even though they were not necessarily always soluble.

These two examples illustrate the difference between informal and formal development processes. They also bring up the issue of the different development needs of different individuals and the different opportunities of meeting those needs. The two managers were roughly the same age when they had these two different, significant learning experiences. A second important point is that although the first manager recognized in retrospect what he had learned, the processes of 'joint problem solving' and 'coaching' were not offered by his boss as part of a formal management development scheme. They were just things he did as part of his normal managerial work.

In reviewing your own experiences, and looking at those of people around you, you are likely to have found a variety of good and bad experiences. You may find either for yourself or for the majority of your colleagues that their careers and successes have been significantly stimulated by planned job moves or excellent courses. You may alternatively find, as I frequently did in my research with directors,[1] that you or your colleagues' most significant learning experiences were not derived from careful planning and structure but from the accidents of working with particular bosses in particular situations and of meeting changing challenges and opportunities.

One major finding of that research was not simply that so many directors identified informal, not formal, experiences. It was how much more frequently informal experiences were quoted even where the individuals concerned had been exposed to courses or worked in organizations with planned job moves. When I talked in my introduction about a 'balanced view of management development' I meant that we have to consider management development as a total process which embraces the informal and accidental as well as the formal.

DEFINITION OF MANAGEMENT DEVELOPMENT

We have to take account of both formal and informal processes for the following reasons:

- Everyone will agree that we learn through informal processes, although the proportion of formal and informal will vary
- If we apply the term management development only to formal processes we are excluding a large part of common experience
- If we exclude a large part of common experience from our definition, and more especially our understanding, of management development, we are doing something more than being potentially illogical: we are being unhelpful to managers by dismissing that part of their learning and development which many of them will recognize most readily and which in their own ways they use most effectively

This separation of formal management development and informal learning is something which existed for me until relatively recently. I used to use a shorter version of a definition of management development produced by the Training Services Agency in 1977: 'an attempt to improve managerial effectiveness through a planned and deliberate learning process'. Yet a great deal of my work had increasingly been on the ways in which managers could learn from opportunities at work in an unplanned, though admittedly thoughtful, way. In *Making experience pay*[2] I described many of these opportunities, but did not sort out in my own mind, let alone offer to other people, a view of whether these processes of learning from practical work experiences could really be included under the kind of definition of management development used by myself and many others.

Of course, it would not matter very much if I, or others, were confused about the scope of management development if this did not affect action. But the fact is that both the definition of management development, and the working practices aimed at meeting that definition, have emphasized formal, planned and deliberate processes which originate from, and are often monitored and controlled by, people and forces other than the individual manager involved.

As your review of your own learning experiences, and your review of the likely answers of others, may well have shown, a great deal of management development is not 'planned and deliberate' – and, even more significantly, probably cannot be. So my revised view of a definition is 'an attempt to improve managerial effectiveness through a learning process'.

The next chapter gives more detail on why the nature of managerial work will always require us to embrace informal and accidental processes of learning in our definition, if we want to tackle the reality of the managerial world rather than to separate ourselves from it.

IS LEARNING DIFFERENT FROM DEVELOPMENT?

Until relatively recently the debate, such as it was, about the possibly different meaning of these two words was really about 'current' versus 'future'. Some people thought that activities directed at performing your current job well involved 'learning', whereas activities aimed at a job or tasks you might do later were really 'development'. More recently an attempt has been made to differentiate the two more on the basis of the content of the experience rather than the present or future application of it. Chris Argyris[3] introduced the idea that the learning necessary to use present processes to meet current job requirements could be closely specified and developed. He saw this as 'single loop learning', as compared with the process of challenging the nature of the problems, redefining them and perhaps transforming the organization and its values, a process he called 'double loop learning'.

Pedler and Boydell[4] distinguish explicitly between learning and development. They see learning as more concerned with an increase in knowledge or a higher degree of an existing skill, whereas development is, in their view, a move towards a different state of being or functioning.

Other authors have argued for the concept of different 'levels' of learning. It is a readily acceptable idea that some things are relatively easy to accept and implement, while others require a greater degree of personal commitment and understanding. While these authors highlight several interesting issues, the most important seem to me to be discussions of the objectives of development processes. The purpose of development or learning is to encourage challenge and debate, either about the nature of the organization or the individual. Do those who offer such opportunities accept the dangers and risks involved, and do they make those to whom they are offering the opportunity aware of those dangers and risks? I do not think that differentiating between 'learning' and 'development' necessarily helps clarify these issues, especially in discussion with managers.

In many ways, it is much more important to note that 'learning' and 'development' are both more relevant terms than 'training' or 'education'. They both say more about output – about results – than input and activity. This last point connects with something Winston Churchill is supposed to have said. 'I am always ready to learn, but I did not always like being taught.' This again says something to us about the likely response of many managers to formal processes, particularly courses. It also takes us, finally, back to the point about management development being essentially a process done *by* you rather than done *to* you. The movement towards self-development as a philosophy and process has been, with action learning, one of the two major changes in understanding about management development in this country in the last fifteen years.

YOUR ORGANIZATION'S EXPERIENCE OF MANAGEMENT DEVELOPMENT

Personnel and management development advisers normally believe in formal management development processes. Providing opportunities for these is often, of course, a stated part of their job description. Their oral comments, written statements and policies, and their actions all suggest they have the following beliefs:

- Managers are not born, they are not made, but they can be developed
- Most managers do not carry out their responsibility for the

development of other managers properly; if left to themselves, not much of value would happen

- It is therefore necessary to set up systems for management development through which the processes of developing managers are organized and planned
- The effectiveness of such systems depends to a very large degree on the commitment of top management; that commitment is often difficult to obtain
- Managers cannot be expected to enjoy the formal disciplines involved in planned development
- The results achieved by planned management development are so obvious that there is no need to set clear objectives and monitor results.

Not all organizations have a personnel director or management development adviser with a clear responsibility for the development of managers. Some small organizations may certainly have an administration director or company secretary who has some interest in, and perhaps responsibility for, formal management development. In a few organizations the lead will be taken not only in principle but in detail by the chief executive. Whatever their job title, however, the beliefs of people trying to initiate or review formal management development processes are likely to be similar to those given above. You can test yourself:

Exercise

How far on a scale 0 = low, 10 = high, do I agree with the statements made above?

If we move from beliefs about the desirability of formal management development processes to actuality, you can look next at how far your organization goes in providing formal management development. Some organizations offer absolutely nothing – no individual reviews, no plans for individual development, no annual review of succession, no nominations for courses. Others provide a full range of formal opportunities. Inevitably a lot are in the middle, providing something but not everything, or providing for lower level managers but not for the most senior. The phrase 'management development' has probably existed in the UK only since 1951. While some commercial and industrial organizations will have been carrying out at least some of the processes identified below for even longer than that, formal management development has been put in place much more recently in most organizations.

ELEMENTS OF FORMAL MANAGEMENT DEVELOPMENT

Formal management development will normally include the following items:

- a statement of the purpose of management development, such as

  to ensure that executives are developed or recruited and trained in sufficient numbers to sufficient standards to meet the specialist and general management requirements of the group in the short and the long term.

(See Figure 1.3 for a more extended version.)

Some organizations will have set and sustained an objective that all top management appointments should be filled from within, from people developed by the organization itself. Others will have set some target figure for recruitment from outside, or will in practice operate a modification whereby senior functional jobs are filled from outside (e.g. finance or personnel).

Even some organizations which have dedicated attention and resources to formal management development do not necessarily have a policy about it. This may be because the organizations concerned have such a well established series of procedures and processes that there is no need to give the attention and focus that the production of a formal policy might achieve. Other organizations have found that the production of a policy document has been valuable precisely because it provides the opportunity for drawing attention to the issue and at least stating what the organization believes.

- a statement about the processes to be used in identifying and developing managers. Characteristically, such a statement will refer to individual performance review or apraisal, to the identification of individual training and development needs, the planning and review processes applying to these individual assessments and perhaps to the decision-making powers of those involved in making job-movement or development decisions.

- appraisal processes and procedures, which will be identified, perhaps with some guidance given in written form – possibly supplemented by training – on how to carry out the review and development task with individuals.
- the range of development processes which might be considered; these may be indicated either on an appraisal form or in a guidance booklet.

Figure 1.3   Management Development Policy

Effective management is clearly vital to the success and continuing prosperity of the group, and to the security and quality of employment and morale of its staff.

We accept that it is the group's responsibility to:
- provide every manager with the opportunity to develop his ability and potential so that he does his existing job effectively
- ensure that there is an adequate supply of trained staff who are competent for promotion to meet the future managerial needs of the group

We believe:
- that people derive more satisfaction from working when they themselves have helped to establish and are committed to the objective of their jobs
- that people should be encouraged to develop their own creative roles, exercise initiative and demonstrate self-discipline within the agreed limits of their jobs

Application
The policy requires that through the divisons:
- we create an environment in which all managers contribute to the objectives of the business to their maximum ability
- we give all managers the scope for exercising initiative by allocating responsibility with authority down the line and see that decisions are taken at the lowest appropriate level
- we ensure that every manager participates with his superior in determining the basic responsibilities of his job, and the results that can be reasonably expected of him, and accepts full responsibility for achieving those results
- we appraise every manager's performance against his expected results, for the purpose of helping him to develop his skills and improve his performance
- we assess every manager's potential on the quality of his performance
- we encourage and train all managers to adopt a similar policy in the management of their subordinates

Context
We have undertaken to support this policy by:
- providing an organizational structure within which the responsibilities of each manager are clearly defined
- providing and implementing consistent personnel policies covering recruitment, salaries and promotion
- providing appropriate training and development programmes

Expectations
We expect that increasing the influence and scope for initiative and self-motivation of managers and their subordinates will lead to increasing job satisfaction and to direct improvement in the group's commercial performance and efficiency

Formal Development Processes

The following processes, normally arranged through the intervention of someone other than the manager and his or her boss, and designed explicitly with a development objective, are 'planned and deliberate learning processes'. All of these might form part of the armoury of any formal management development system, in the sense that they could be considered, recommended or applied by advisers, bosses or by individuals themselves.

Changes in job and job content

- promotion to a new job
- movement to a job at a similar level but in a different function, product or activity (job rotation)
- stretching the boundaries of a job by allocating additional responsibilities or tasks
- secondment, i.e. (in my definition) movement outside the employing oranization to a different job
- special projects, i.e. (in my definition) being given responsibility for a special project outside the normal routines of current job
- committees or task groups where the content of what was being studied would normally be within the current experience and competence of the manager involved; sometimes the content would, however, be outside his current job in terms of level or function
- junior boards, set up to 'preview' decisions required by the board proper.

Development processes within the job
Formal development interventions include:

- coaching, i.e. being deliberately taken through problems and issues with the explicit intention of developing the recipient (this is usually carried out by the boss)
- counselling, often carried out in the context of an appraisal or performance review, and involving either specific counselling and advice about a particular aspect of performance, or occasionally personality or longer-term career guidance (again usually carried out by the boss)
- monitoring and feedback by boss

- mentoring (in my definition) undertaken by someone other than the manager's direct boss. This is an advisory relationship between a manager and, usually, a respected senior individual who provides guidance and advice on processes, organizational policies and the way to do things generally. It may involve a respected senior presenting the case for a candidate for a particular job

Activities external to the job
These include:

- internal courses
- external courses
- work on external committees, associations, voluntary or charity organizations
- reading

Development activities planned by the individual

- modelling on boss, colleagues or outsiders
- reading
- participation in groups of managers from different organizations

WHERE ARE YOU?

Exercise

You can assess your organization on each of the elements and each of the processes. Which of them exist or are used? Again, you can use a scale of 0 = low, 10 = high.

You may, of course, work for an organization with relatively autonomous units, some of which may achieve a high score on this analysis and others a low score. You might therefore like to consider these questions for different units.

You may wish to take your analysis further by considering the reasons for the scores you have given, whether for your organization as a whole or for particular units. Sometimes an organization has simply not considered some part of the formal opportunities that exist or can be created. Sometimes it has tried the process, or a version of it, in the past and found that it did not work. Sometimes the opportunities simply cannot be created.

Finally, it may be worth carrying out your analysis according to some definition of the levels of manager who might be involved. It is frequently the case, for example, that courses are more readily made available to lower levels of management, and certainly that senior levels go on external courses only, if they go on courses at all. We found in our research with directors, which confirmed our own working experience, that the senior levels of an organization are much less likely to be subject to appraisal as a formal process than are middle and lower levels.

One of the positive results of Professor Charles Handy's report *The making of managers*[5] was the development of the Management Charter initiative (see Chapter 12 for more information). The idea that organizations should voluntarily commit themselves to good management development practices, and share these with other organizations, was expressed formally in a code of practice (Figure 1.4). At the time of writing this book something like 200 organizations had formally subscribed to this Charter. It is an alternative, though less detailed, way of reviewing where your organization is. Work out to what extent you could legitimately say you are already doing the things mentioned in the Charter.

THE LEARNING CULTURE OF AN ORGANIZATION

The list of formal processes you have considered is fairly clear cut: responses can be based on hard facts. An alternative approach is to consider what the organization 'feels like' in terms of its encouragement of learning and development. It is also possible to widen your analysis of the organization beyond the formal processes illustrated above. Here is a checklist to enable you to do this.

An organization can be said to encourage learning when:

- it encourages managers to identify their own learning needs
- it provides a regular review of performance and learning for the individual
- it encourages managers to set challenging learning goals for themselves
- it provides feedback at the time on both performance and achieved learning
- it reviews the performance of managers in helping to develop others

- it assists managers to see learning opportunities on the job
- it seeks to provide new experiences from which managers can learn
- it provides or facilitates the use of training on the job
- it tolerates some mistakes, provided managers try to learn from them
- it encourages managers to review, conclude and plan learning activities
- it encourages managers to challenge the traditional ways of doing things.

Figure 1.4   The Management Charter – A Code of Practice

We recognize that good management practice is essential if we are to maximize the potential of our most valuable resource: the people who work here. Their enterprise, initiative and creativity is crucial to our future success.

We are therefore committed to the following:

- to improve leadership and management skills throughout the organization
- to encourage and support our managers in continuously developing management skills and leadership qualities in themselves and in those with whom they work
- to back this by providing a coherent framework for self-development – within the context of our corporate goals – which is understood by those concerned and in which they play an active part
- to ensure that the development of managerial expertise is a continuous process and will be integrated with the work flow of the organization
- to provide ready access to the relevant learning and development opportunities – internal and external – with requisite support and time released, appropriate to our organization
- to encourage and help managers to acquire recognized qualifications relevant both to their personal development and to our corporate goals
- to participate actively in the appropriate networks of the Management Charter initiative and thereby share information, ideas, experience, expertise and resources that will prove mutually beneficial to the participants and help us to further the aims of this code
- directly and through networks, to strengthen our links with sources of management education to ensure that the training offered best complements our management development programmes, matching our corporate needs and future requirements
- to contribute to closer links with local educational establishments to promote a clear understanding of the role of management, its challenge as a career and the excellent opportunities for young people to develop professionalism in its practice
- to appoint a director or equivalent to oversee the fulfilment of these undertakings; to review our progress annually and, after evaluating the contribution to our performance, set new targets for both individuals and the organization; and to publicize highlights from the review and the new targets

Chief executives should undertake to communicate and demonstrate to all managers their commitment to the above code.

Exercise

Review each of the factors listed on pages 13–14 for your organization and mark on a scale 0 = low, 10 = high the extent to which you believe the criteria to be currently met.

WHERE ARE WE? – A COMPANY CASE

I was asked to carry out a review of the management development policies and processes of a large UK-based company. It had been active in formal management development for thirty years. I reviewed the documents, plans, processes and brochures available from its files and interviewed a number of personnel staff. I generated the following questions which I discussed with twenty senior managers and directors.

Exercise

1 What do you believe to be the purpose of the company's management development policies? How effective have they been for yourself and for the managers reporting to you?
2 How helpful has the appraisal process been in defining the effectiveness of individual managers and their development needs?
3 Do you use other processes for reviewing performance and development?
4 Do you believe that the processes for collecting and reviewing individual potential have worked satisfactorily, e.g. succession planning?
5 What contribution has been made by processes such as job rotation, internal or external courses?
6 Can you quote cases of managers who are more effective as a result of these management development processes?

What would the answers be in your organization?

WHO THINKS WHAT?

The last case study enabled me to carry out at much greater depth and with a much larger number of people the process which I had employed in my original research with directors. We were able to compare what the organization said it had been trying to do with what it was perceived to have achieved by the respondent managers and directors. The organizational view was normally given by the chief executive or, in larger organizations, by the personnel director and management development adviser, as in the case quoted above. The comparisons we were able to make between these two sources of evidence were powerful and disturbing.

The question of ownership raises one of the most significant issues. It is normally part of the stated values of the modern personnel practitioner that desirable management practices, in this case a management development scheme, should be 'owned' by line managers rather than by personnel. In fact, while personnel people certainly want line management to 'own' the management development scheme, they frequently have great difficulty in actually securing a transfer. They commonly ascribe this to the failure of line managers to recognize how important such issues are.

In a sense the personnel people are right – line managers often do not want to participate in the disciplines of the formal management development process. However, you might benefit from asking yourself the following questions.

Exercise

1   Who really 'owns' our management development scheme? How do they demonstrate their ownership?
2   If we in personnel are really the initiators, proponents and monitors of the management development scheme, why has this happened?
3   Could it be that line managers do not own the scheme because they do not see it as dealing with their major business concerns? Could it be that they see the scheme as being about some expensive technique called 'management development', rather than about how managers learn?

These latter stages in your self-analysis should help you to focus on two important aspects of knowing where you are starting from. It is quite likely that both you and your managers have

currently considered only 'planned and deliberate learning processes' as proper management development. Understandably, these
processes are considered by both personnel and line managers to
be the appropriate responsibility of the people seen to be professional
in 'planned and deliberate learning processes'. If these formal
processes are the only things on which you and your organizational
clients want to concentrate, then you should find my checklists on
formal issues mentioned above useful and helpful. You may also
find that you want to move from this chapter to those chapters
which deal explicitly with the formal processes, especially Chapters
6, 7 and 8.

THE BELIEFS OF CHIEF EXECUTIVES

The review of the beliefs of personnel people on pages 7–8
included a statement about the importance of commitment by top
management. The bad news is that such commitment is difficult
to obtain; all too frequently lip-service is paid at best. For example,
chief executives are much more likely to sign the annual letter
starting the round of appraisals than they are actually to appraise
their own direct subordinates. The good news is that a great deal
of effective management development can be achieved without the
direct help of the chief executive. In terms of testing where you
are, however, it might well be helpful to look at the beliefs of your
chief executive or relevant head of your organizational unit. We
are fortunate in being able to compare individual chief executive
opinions with those found by Charles Margerison in the UK. His
study was replicated with very similar results in the United States.[6]
The research asked chief executives to identify the major influences
which had helped them develop as managers. The results are given
in Figure 1.5.

As a starting proposition we could conclude that if these are
the beliefs that chief executives had about what influenced their
progress, they might be likely to apply those beliefs to the
development of their subordinate managers. In analysing your own
organizational level it could be valuable to make your assessment
of where your chief executive stands on this list. Would you place
things in the same order of priority?

Two cautionary comments are desirable. The process used for
collecting this information – questionnaires – is different from that
used in my own research through live interviews. It may be that
individuals respond differently to questionnaires as compared to

Figure 1.5   Reported Major Influences on Chief Executives

Rank order	Statements	Score out of 100
1	Ability to work with a wide variety of people	78.4
2	Early overall responsibility for important tasks	74.8
3	A need to achieve results	74.8
4	Leadership experience early in career	73.6
5	Wide experience in many functions before 35	67.6
6	An ability to do deals and negotiate	66.4
7	Willingness to take risks	62.8
8	Having more ideas than other colleagues	61.6
9	Being stretched by immediate bosses	60.4
10	An ability to change managerial style to suit occasion	58.8
11	A desire to seek new opportunities	56.8
12	Becoming visible to top management before 30	56.0
13	Family support (wife/parents)	55.2
14	Having a sound technical training	54.8
15	Having a manager early in your career who acted as a model (from whom you learnt a lot)	52.0
16	Overseas managerial/work experience	41.2
17	Experience of leadership in armed forces (peacetime/wartime)	40.4
18	Having special 'off the job' management training	32.8

interviews. If you were thinking of getting your own chief executive to fill in such a chart, you might have to balance the apparent ease and speed of that kind of process with the advantages of a biographical discussion. Secondly, there is a risk in the statement with which I started this section. It may seem reasonable to assume that the actions or views of chief executives would reflect their beliefs about management development processes. There are, however, two good reasons for supposing this may not be true. The first is one to which I have already referred in relation to personnel people themselves. People often have values which they do not actually adhere to in practice. Anyone whose experience inclines them to disbelieve this statement is referred to the marvellous case study given by Chris Argyris on appraisal.[7]

The second reason for looking closely at this list takes us back to the point of doing it in the first place. My suggestion was that you should analyse a particular chief executive – indeed, that you might ask a chief executive to do it for him or herself. You want to establish the actual position of your own chief executive, which may differ from the general views of this sample. You want to know whether your particular chief executive favours 'early overall responsibility for important tasks'.

With all these qualifications, Charles Margerison's list provides a potentially helpful aid to establishing where you are.

SOME FINAL QUESTIONS

I have included a number of exercises and questions in the body of the chapter. Here are some more questions and some suggestions for action.

The final question on where you are is directed at those organizations which have a personnel specialist, particularly a management development adviser. The attention which organizations pay to management development is doubly related to the organizational position of those who advise on management development. If the organization is serious then status will follow – but of course if you do not have status it is difficult to persuade the organization to be serious! It is easy to blame the organization for having low status management development advisers; but may the low status not be a reflection of the processes which they try to sell?

Exercise

1   What have I learned about myself as a learner? What conclusions do I draw for myself and in relation to others?
2   What has been the balance of formal as compared with informal processes for myself? How has this influenced what I offer the organization?
3   Where do I stand on the lists of beliefs about formal management development given on pages 7–8? Is there anything in this chapter which causes me to change those views?
4   Could I use one of the organizational audit checklists? or several? How?
5   How could I compare my own answers on any of these exercises with those of:
    ● another person in my own function within my own organization?
    ● a line manager in my own organization?
    ● a friendly outsider?
6   What definition of management development did I hold before reading this chapter? Has this reading changed it? If so, what kind of action might I take?
7   Do I see management development as concerned with remedying weaknesses, developing potential or both? Would my answers be the same for everyone or different for different managers?
8   If asked to assess the success of formal management development processes in my organization, what answer would I give?

9	To what would I attribute the level of success on formal manage-
ment development processes:
* the enthusiasm and commitment of top management?
* the content of the scheme?
* my own involvement and influence?
* the involvement and influence of my predecessor?

REFERENCES

1	MUMFORD A. *Developing top managers*. Gower, 1988
2	MUMFORD A. *Making experience pay*. McGraw Hill, 1980
3	ARGYRIS C. 'Double loop learning in organisations'. *Harvard Business Review*. September/October 1977
4	PEDLER M. and BOYDELL T. *Managing yourself*. Fontana, 1985
5	HANDY C. *The making of managers*. NEDO, 1987
6	MARGERISON C. 'How chief executives succeed'. *Journal of European Industrial Training*. Vol 4, No 5, 1980; MARGERISON, C. and KAKABADSE, A. *How American executives succeed*. American Management Association, 1984.
7	ARGYRIS C. *Reasoning, learning and action*. Jossey Bass, 1982

2 Management Development Models

Current definitions of management development, and much of the formal practice in response, have been flawed. An over-emphasis on the 'planned and deliberate' has excluded many of the experiences which are particularly real for managers. The exclusion of those preponderant and powerful experiences is not only illogical but leads to a diminished persuasiveness in talking to managers about development. We have therefore reached a position in which the reality of management development is reversed, so that the minority pursuits of carefully planned and deliberate development experiences have become the only ones recognized as management development! This creates an *Alice in Wonderland* situation, where Humpty Dumpty says 'words mean what I say they mean'.

This unreal position has been arrived at for entirely under-standable and laudable reasons. Explicit, powerful, relevant, realistic – these are all appropriate words to use about the unplan-ned experiences which managers so often quote as the main source of their development. Yet the same experiences are fragmentary, insufficient, inefficient, only partially understood and subject to the winds of circumstance.

It is also understandable that personnel and management development advisers intervene on what they feel themselves able to deal with. It is quite understandable that they put aside those uncontrolled, day-by-day, accidental and frenetic activities from which managers claim to learn. It is quite logical for them to prefer to deal rather with processes and exercises over which they have influence and indeed often power, which they can claim to understand and rationalize and which represent a defined area of their own territory. However, one of the consequences is that they then set up a game which is different from the one managers

normally play in and in which personnel and management development people use rules which are also quite different from those
which obtain in normal managerial work.

There are a number of reasons why formal management
development processes have not worked successfully in many
organizations. Here it is necessary to establish only that formal
management development processes, often owned by personnel
people and not line managers, have not become part of managers'
own understanding of learning and development.

It is also true that personnel people have been insufficiently
attached to the reality of managerial work. For thirty years formal
management training and education has sought to improve the
reality of its products. It has moved from lectures by more or
less authoritative people to syndicate discussions in which groups
of managers exchange comments and experiences. When these
discussions were found to be lacking in both reality and intellectual stimulus – so that the syndicates could be defined as groups
gathered together to exchange ignorance – they were replaced by
case studies on the Harvard method. When case studies were
found to be productive of analytical thought but lacking the
tensions of immediate cut and thrust (except when conducted by
a charismatic tutor), increased emphasis was given to a variety of
simulations. In these processes, whether building bridges or
towers in Lego bricks, constructing paper planes, doing computer-
ized business exercises or engaging in the latest fashion for outdoor training, the basic intention was normally to reproduce the
tensions created by the pressures of time, conflicting priorities
and not always helpful colleagues. In developing courses there
has been a continuing search for techniques which could be
employed to improve the reality of the process.

It took the coincidence of a series of events connecting the
creation of Manchester Business School, the departure of Reg
Revans and his creation of the first major action learning programme in Belgium, and Lord Weinstock having 'flu and watching television, for the major breakthrough of action learning to
be achieved and recognized. Revans developed the proposition
that managers preferred to work on and discuss real issues rather
than participate in traditional courses. In essence his process not
only uses the recognition that managers learn most from working
on real management problems, but faces management educators
and trainers with the proposition that the construction of neat
separate boxes of learning experiences, even simulations, is unnecessary.

Revans is the extreme manifestation of the desire to take management development back into the reality of management. The separation of learning experiences from work experiences is:

- illogical
- unreal
- unhelpful
- unnecessary

I have confessed that until recently I managed to work on both formal and informal aspects of management development without fully recognizing the necessity of drawing them together. I have come to recognize, however, that it is not appropriate to operate powerfully and apparently effectively in one area unless this can be integrated with the other. Although, as I will show, it is highly desirable that formal processes deal confidently and explicitly with the reality of managerial life rather than with some academic view of what it ought to be, the incoherent and barely recognized learning that people achieve from *ad hoc* work experiences is disastrously insufficient. We must have an understanding of management development which provides a complete model of the total process, not only the formal part of it. Just as we need to increase the reality of formal off-the-job development, so we need to increase the capacity to learn from informal experiences at work.

DEFINING REALITY IN MANAGEMENT

So we ought to incorporate both formal and informal processes in any definition of, and practical work towards, improved management development. I have so far made the case purely in terms of the fact that managers learn in a variety of informal and often unconscious ways. The attempt to concentrate entirely on the formal processes, although initially understandable in terms of the obvious inefficiencies of informal development, has been misconceived for another reason.

The separation of formal management development from informal processes literally takes management development away from the reality of on-the-job managerial work. The planning of job moves for development purposes, or the development and implementation of training and education, are divorced in terms of time, mental application and even physical circumstances from

managers' normal activities. Although this is done for the apparently
best of motivations – the hit-and-miss nature and inefficiency of
on-the-job learning processes – the result has been the construction
of management development processes and activities which are not
seen by managers as part of their real world.

In addition to the failure to identify and make use of the full
range of development processes, both on the job and off the job,
another reason why the balance of attention has been fixed so
firmly on the formal derives from inappropriate and obsolete
models of what managers actually do. We can only be surprised
and saddened by the continuing apparent failure of many authors,
business schools and management training centres to define and
implement their offerings in terms of what managers actually do.
Rosemary Stewart's fundamental work[1] has, it seems, been adopted
neither by management developers nor by management educators
and trainers. Henry Mintzberg's[2] analysis of managerial roles
appears rather more frequently on courses; but again the fundamental features of managerial life which he identified have not apparently
affected the philosophy or major substance of development programmes or courses. At best his chart has been used to provide an
interesting session. Nor has the work of John Kotter,[3] similarly
powerful in exhibiting the realities of what top managers do,
influenced management developers as yet.

The results of these research studies are developed in Chapter
6, which looks in more detail at the things managers have to do
well as the necessary focus of development activities. Here the
fundamental point is that all the research on what managers actually
do points in the same direction. Their work is carried out at a
hectic pace, it is fragmented, it is more likely to be intuitive and
responsive than rational and reflective. Perhaps most important of
all, what managers actually need to be able to do is more likely to
be specific and contingent than easily generalizable.

Although there are common aspects to managerial jobs, it is
the particularities which often represent the greater challenge. The
view that a good manager can manage anything is not a good
prescription either for career development or for the construction
of management development schemes. There are elements of
managerial effectiveness in common between the work of a reseach
manager and that of a sales manager; but the reality of effective
development for these two jobs is likely to be very different. This
is true not only for the obvious professional and functional
differences. It is even true for something which may seem to be
appropriately generalizable. Since one of the characteristics of a

manager is that she or he manages people, one of the more generalizable aspects would seem to be the process of delegation. Yet if we take sales and research managers, the probability is that effective delegation in these two jobs would be quite different, not only in terms of what is delegated but perhaps even more importantly, how it is delegated.

Management development ought, then, to be based on:

- a wide view of development processes, accepting the reality of the ways in which managers will learn
- the relatively disorganized reality of managerial work, as compared with the neatness of classical management theory
- the particulars of what managers have to do in specific jobs within different kinds of organization

The argument is not that it is inappropriate to help managers to be more systematic, better organized or more reflective. It is a very appropriate purpose of management development to challenge and stimulate improvement even among managers who work relatively effectively, let alone among that considerable number who work very ineffectively. The case is rather that management development must recognize and make use of the relatively chaotic and unplanned nature of a great deal of management instead of ignoring it or attempting to replace it with formal management development alone.

One final implication emerges from the research and from my own and others' experience over the years. Managers are people who actually do things and get others to do things. Their prime concern is normally to implement effective action rather than to collect knowledge for its own sake. The understandable tendency of management academics and theorists and, indeed, of some managerial authors, is to create neat boxes, clear statements, to distinguish one kind of action, one function, one form of behaviour from another. As an analytical process this is understandable and, up to a point, useful. But most managers operate as if they were multi-programmed. They do not concentrate on one thing at a time, applying the knowledge that they have acquired in a discrete way. They work on a complex tangle of issues and their prime purpose is to achieve an end result. What they achieve may occasionally surprise them as much as it may bewilder others. The important point is that they *do* achieve things. A development process which is focused on the acquisition of knowledge (however seductively organized the knowledge-gathering process is) is there-

fore likely to be less helpful than one which emphasizes what
managers have to do in order to be effective, and how they do it.

As a concrete illustration of this point, consider the implications
of one of the most important findings of the three researchers
mentioned above. One of the major factors contributing to the
effectiveness of managers is their use of networks. It would therefore
be logical if management development processes were geared to
helping managers identify and use those networks successfully, for
example through identifying the kind of behaviours in which they
need to engage. One of the more familiar traditional management
development objectives is to give managers knowledge about other
functions. Traditional management development, for example,
exposes production managers to a knowledge of marketing processes. It is believed that the acquisition of such knowledge will
somehow improve relationships between them. A management
development process which focused on effectiveness would instead
deal with the issue of the systems through which these two
departments interact, the basis of relationships between the two
departments in pursuing their objectives and how these could be
improved. Although it may undoubtedly at some level be a useful
piece of knowledge for the production manager to know how the
marketing manager produces a marketing plan, in real managerial
life the more important issue is how the production manager
and marketing manager develop a process for managing the
consequences of the plan.

EFFECTIVENESS IN LEARNING PROCESSES

There is a third major input to the creation of effective management
development. Even if our conceptual understanding, and our
practical application of our management development scheme, were
to include the widest variety of development processes and focus
clearly on what managers really do, we would not have provided all
that is necessary for effective development. To expose managers to a
variety of developmental opportunities, and to base more of them in
different ways on real managerial processes, is certainly likely to
raise the general level of achievement. On their own, however, these
two processes will not transform traditional understanding about
management development. A third element is the process of learning
and development itself. The fundamental point here is that past

generalization about how managers learn has been found to be as badly flawed as some of the other generalizations we have been examining. Over a thirty-year period there has been a fairly consistent search for activities which can be seen not only as real, but which in some sense 'involve' managers and require them to 'participate'. The grotesque ineffectiveness of the lecture process, and the vociferous feedback of many managers bored with being its victims, has led to the development of a variety of teaching methods, and particularly of active simulations. In the course context this has meant that most course designers have tried to provide a variety of processes. This was partly because variety was seen as a good thing in itself, since managers would be more likely to remain interested if they were offered a varied process. But it also stemmed from partial recognition of a much more fundamental point.

More aware tutors frequently find themselves faced with conflicting feedback. A session marked very highly by some managers will be marked poorly by others. A process found particularly stimulating by some will be put down as wholly unreal by others. A stimulating and charismatic lecturer will be marked as the highlight of a course by some managers and rejected by others as having had 'nothing concrete to say about my kind of organization'. The result of conflicting feedback of this kind over years of experience has led at least some tutors to provide 'the catholic menu'. This means providing a variety of experiences because you know that some participants will enjoy one form of learning whereas others will not. The catholic menu provides the course designer with a basic protection: not all participants will be bored all of the time.

It ought to come as no surprise at all that managers differ in their likely response to any particular learning process. Not only is this our common experience within the formal learning environment; it is also observably true that managers differ in their ability to learn from particular kinds of opportunity on the job. We face a remarkably self-evident conclusion. People differ in their preferences for opera and pop music, for different kinds of sporting activity, in their enjoyment of different holidays. Closer to home, in management development terms we know that managers differ substantially in terms of managerial style. Some are hard-edged, directive, forceful autocrats, some are reflective and listening people who prefer to consult before making a decision. So it should be no surprise to us that people differ in their preferred approach to learning. The question for management development is what you are prepared to do about such differences.

The answer to that question has often been a sort of unfocused general provision where it is hoped that the offer of a wide range of different kinds of opportunity or process will mean that successes are balanced by failures. A really effective management development model can, and should, go much further than this. The stimulus to my own thinking beyond 'people learn differently' was provided when I first encountered the work of David Kolb. At the theoretical and conceptual level his ideas are available in his major book.[4] He would not, I think, claim that his concept of the learning cycle was wholly new. His startling and most useful innovation was to show that it is possible to use a diagnostic instrument to identify which people were likely to have a preference for which kind of learning activity within the learning cycle.

Peter Honey and I took Kolb's original concepts and developed a different questionnaire and improved processes for making use of the results. The full detail of our work on learning styles is available elsewhere.[5] A brief summary of our major conclusions, and of the impact of these on the design of effective management development, is now necessary.

Figure 2.1   Honey and Mumford's Learning Cycle

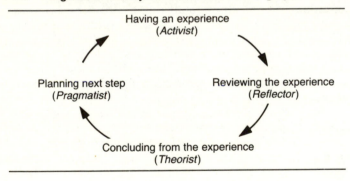

Having an experience
(*Activist*)

Reviewing the experience
(*Reflector*)

Concluding from the experience
(*Theorist*)

Planning next step
(*Pragmatist*)

THE LEARNING CYCLE

All managerial learning involves all stages of the cycle (see Figure 2.1); the emphasis will differ for particular kinds of activity. Reading a book is having an experience; but so is working on a major business project for six months.

While the emphasis given to parts of the cycle may differ according to the nature of the experience, they may also observably differ not because of the objective nature of the activity but because of the personal preference and ability of the learner. The anecdotal discovery that individuals differ in terms of their receptiveness to particular kinds of learning process can be explained in terms of their relative preference for, or rejection of, a particular stage on the learning cycle. Four major styles are identifiable not only through the Learning Styles Questionnaire but by observation and by self-analysis and perception.

Activists:

- try anything once
- tend to revel in short-term crises, firefighting
- tend to thrive on the challenge of new experiences
- are relatively bored with implementation and longer-term consolidation
- constantly involve themselves with other people

Reflectors:

- like to stand back and review experiences from different perspectives
- collect data and analyse it before coming to conclusions
- like to consider all possible angles and implications before making a move
- tend to be cautious
- actually enjoy observing other people in action
- often take a back seat at meetings

Theorists:

- are keen on basic assumptions, principles, theories, models and systems thinking
- prize rationality and logic
- tend to be detached and analytical
- are unhappy with subjective or ambiguous experiences
- like to make things tidy and fit them into rational schemes

Pragmatists:

- positively search out new ideas or techniques which might apply in their situation
- take the first opportunity to experiment with applications

- respond to problems and opportunities 'as a challenge'
- are keen to use ideas from management courses
- like to get on with things with clear purpose

The detailed application of this kind of knowledge is covered in later chapters, which deal, for example, with the issue of how far you can go in providing different learning processes for individuals with different preferences. From the perspective of this chapter the important point to emphasize is that only 20 per cent of managers emerged with three strong preferences, i.e. could be seen as potentially good all-round learners. In contrast, 35 per cent of managers had one strong preference. An effective management development scheme must take account of the fact that individuals will respond differently to the same kind of learning opportunity, whether part of a real task or a course.

THE TRIANGLE OF EFFECTIVENESS

The three issues I have been discussing so far all provide for effectiveness. Three points can be usefully presented visually, as in

Figure 2.2   Effectiveness Triangle in Management Development

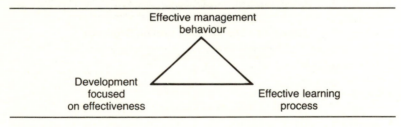

Figure 2.2. The point, literally, of the triangle is that the purpose of management development is not to have a particular kind of development, nor even to provide an effective learning process, but that these two both focus on and are pointed towards effective managerial behaviour.

VIRTUOUS AND VICIOUS LEARNING SEQUENCES

Modern motivational theory tells us that behaviour which is not rewarded is not willingly repeated. Clearly, some managers have had useful management training or educational experiences and subsequently repeat these experiences. There are at least an equivalent number who have had bad experiences which have put them off formal management training or education.

What we have just been looking at in terms of the reality of management impacts specifically on the effectiveness of any learning experience. It can be shown diagramatically in Figures 2.3 and 2.4.

Figure 2.3   The Virtuous Learning Circle

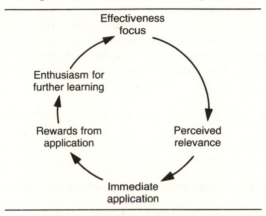

Figure 2.4   The Vicious Learning Sequence

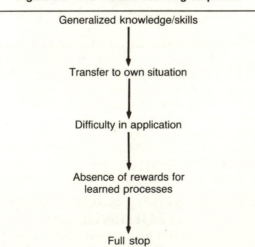

The virtuous learning circle helps us to understand the most powerful and significant statement about management development in the 1970s, made by Reg Revans in *Action learning*.[6] Revans himself has never attempted to provide a single statement which encompasses all his views about action learning. From a review of his many books and papers and those of other followers. I have generated the summary which follows.

A REVIEW OF ACTION LEARNING

- Learning for managers should mean learning to take effective action. Acquiring information, becoming more capable in diagnosis or analysis has been overvalued in management learning.
- Learning to take action necessarily involves actually taking action, not recommending action or undertaking analyses of someone else's problem.
- The best form of action for learning is work on a defined project of reality and significance to managers themselves. The project should involve implementation as well as analysis and recommendation.
- While managers should have responsibility for their own achievements on their own projects, the learning process is a social one: managers learn best with and from each other.
- The social process is achieved and managed through regular meetings of managers to discuss their individual projects; the group is usually called a 'set'. The managers are 'comrades in adversity'.
- The role of people providing help for the members of the set is essentially and crucially different from that of the normal management teacher. Their role is not to teach (whether through lecture, case or simulation) but to help managers learn from exposure to problems and to each other. As Revans says, action learning attacks 'the inveterate hankering of the teacher to be the centre of attention'.

Although Revans is primarily associated with action learning, he produced a neat equation describing the total potential managerial learning process, $L = P + Q$. Learning, L, was produced as the result of both programmed knowledge, P, and Q, which is the pursuit of hitherto unresolved questions and problems (the action learning element). Despite his trumpet blasts against the walls of the traditional management development establishment, Revans is not opposed in principle to the virtues of programmed knowledge. He is indeed contemptuous about some aspects of both content and delivery, and certainly about issues of priority. It is obviously true for him that the Q element is both objectively more important and subjectively more attractive to real working managers.

It was probably inevitable that Revans's major contribution would be abused and misused. The crucial point for this chapter is to be found in his focus on learning from doing real work, but doing so in a relatively structured learning environment. The idea of using projects and learning vehicles may well have pre-dated Revans, but the idea existed previously in a significantly different form. The use of a project where a manager operates as a consultant to another organization, or the creation of a project essentially as a simulation exercise within a course context – for example asking course members to 'produce a corporate strategy for the year 1995' – is actually quite different from action learning. To achieve full experiential reality the project must carry real management responsibility and involvement in implementation. This is absolutely fundamental. Some people have been seduced into offering projects which are not 'real work' as I define it. Some are seduced in the opposite direction to offer projects which do involve real work but pay little attention to the learning process. Action learning is not itself a model of management development and can certainly be misused even as a partial answer to some important issues in management development. The Revans equation $L = P + Q$ is a complete model, but is obviously somewhat lacking in detail.

THE MUMFORD MODEL OF MANAGEMENT DEVELOPMENT

My research on how directors learned, the obligation to write a report on it and then the opportunity to write a book helped to sharpen my own conceptual grasp of the totality of management development. Formal management development processes are important but by definition, in the managerial world, insufficient. They are also often inefficiently provided. Informal processes are both insufficient and inefficient, because managers have often lacked the skills to make the most of them as learning experiences. Professionals from the management development world have compounded this failure by paying too little attention to the opportunities informal experiences provide. What we found in our research was that the process of actually asking people about their learning experiences achieved two things (other than contributing factual data to our research): for the people with whom we were having discussions, it brought out the content of, and the processes in, their actual learning experiences; and these discussions and revelations about content and process were the equivalent of a cartoon light bulb shining in the head. If people could clarify their learning experiences in discussion with us, and could identify future potential experiences for themselves and others, was there not some other way of achieving this apart from an accidental visit from a researcher?

I was therefore persuaded of more than the need for a conceptual model of management development which included both informal and formal learning experiences. It was brought home to me that my own writing about better development on the job by a more considered process in fact represented a major third element in such a model. Instead of seeing things simply as either brought about by formal management development pro-cesses, or by accidental, informal, not very effective learning, we should see management development as including improved learning on the job, where the improvement was initiated and sustained by the managers themselves, not by management develop-ment professionals. This was the origin of the model in Figure 2.5. Type 1 learning is likely to be most effective because it is drawn directly from managerial performance. However, from a learning point of view, the emphasis in learning-cycle terms is almost always on the 'having an experience' stage, omitting, certainly as far as conscious processes are concerned, the 'reviewing' stage. Managers subsequently act, so they have in a sense passed through the concluding and planning stages, but all too often experiences which have not been reviewed are not even partially developed as achieved learning.

Nor have the formal development experiences of Type 3 often encouraged or facilitated full learning cycles. Some emphasize altogether too much the delivery of conclusions from other people's experience – lectures, books, case studies. Some supposedly planned management development experiences – such as job rotation – stick at the top of the cycle, again simply offering an experience with no opportunity to reflect on, for example, what working in a different department actually involves. Some formal training cour-ses have, in the pursuit of apparent participation and activity, emphasized the experience stage but really done nothing to facilitate the other three parts of the cycle. In what sense has success or

Figure 2.5   Model of Types of Management Development

Type 1 Informal managerial – accidental processes

Characteristics	Occur within managerial activities
	Explicit intention is task performance
	No clear development objectives
	Unstructured in development terms
	Not planned in advance
	Owned by managers
Development consequences	Learning is real, direct, unconscious, insufficient

Type 2 Integrated managerial – opportunistic processes

Characteristics	Occur within managerial activities
	Explicit intention both task performance and development
	Clear development objectives
	Structured for development by boss and subordinate
	Planned beforehand or reviewed subsequently as learning experiences
	Owned by managers
Development consequences	Learning is real, direct, conscious, more substantial

Type 3 Formal management development – planned processes

Characteristics	Often away from normal managerial activities
	Explicit intention is development
	Clear development objectives
	Structured for development by developers
	Planned beforehand and reviewed subsequently as learning experiences
	Owned more by developers than managers
Development consequences	Learning may be real (through a job) or detached (through a course)
	Is more likely to be conscious, relatively infrequent

---

failure in building a tower of Lego bricks been assimilated as a learning experience rather than enjoyed as an active time filler?

In learning-cycle terms Type 2 attempts to provide precisely that opportunity to review, conclude, plan, act again, review and plan, which we know managers do not normally undertake.

LEVERS FOR SUCCESS, CAUSES OF FAILURE

The first question to ask in considering whether management development is successful or otherwise in your organization is what that term means to you. If you see management development wholly in terms of its formal aspects, then you will want to measure it against criteria appropriate to that definition; if you take the broader view offered here then you will have additional criteria. If you accept my arguments your chances of success will be increased by the increased reality of what you do.

It is explicit in my view of success that management development is actually about improved managerial performance. This may well be difficult to assess because a lot of other variables will also affect managerial performance. The crucial point is that management development should aim directly at managerial effectiveness and be dedicated in terms of priorities and clear intentions to that end. This is different from dedication to, and an attempt to measure, *systems* of management development. The difference becomes clear when you consider alternative answers in discussions I have had with management development advisers. Both the following comments arose in response to my question to advisers on how they measured the success of their Management Development schemes.

Case 1

We have very clear processes set up here. There is Annual Appraisal, and we monitor that the forms have been completed and returned to us. Then we put a lot of effort into reviewing the training and development suggestions included in those forms. For example we decide how many courses we will run on particular subjects from this analysis. We chase up the laggards, but we do not have very many. We also insist that there is some comment in each division's annual business plan on management development. If the plan does not include something it is sent back to them. We send round a catalogue of courses each year, and we also make recommendations about which external courses are appropriate for which levels. We have a written management development policy which says that all managers should be given the opportunity to go on a relevant management training event, and we have recently added a specific target of five days' management training a year.

Case 2

We provide formal encouragement. There is a written policy, and every manager should have a Performance and Development Review at least once a year. But really most of the important work is done by discussion that comes out of our involvement with business plans and problems. Of course it is a good thing to stimulate a general review of management development issues at least once a year at the same time as the Business Plan. But we find most of our real work is done outside that. We try and get managers to think about development opportunities for themselves and for other people at the time they are making their ongoing business decisions. It does not work with all managers, but most actually do work quite well on using the opportunities that emerge from real work problems. A lot of managers prefer to work that way, rather than having theoretical discussions about problems or projects that might come up in the future. But we do not treat them as alternatives – we have a go at both. In fact working successfully through current problems tends to encourage managers then to think about ways in which they can plan ahead a bit. The main thing is to try and stimulate the discussion through the things they are

Figure 2.6   Management Development: Levers for Success

- Clear appropriate job objectives
- Effective selection for the job
- Driven by business opportunities/problems
- Ownership shared
  - hierarchically
  - by individual self-development
  - by personnel
- Shared diagnosis
  - of individual needs
  - of group needs
- Development activities are
  - appropriate to need
  - appropriate to individual
  - based on management reality
- Development processes are linked
- Learning processes are identified and worked on
- Outputs are identified and measured

Figure 2.7   Management Development: Causes of Failure

- Purposes — unclear
            — unsupported by managers
- Poor diagnosis of culture and business requirements
- Poor analysis of individual needs
- Development processes
    — unconvincing to managers
    — inappropriate to need
    — unreal
    — unacceptable to individual
- Overemphasis on
    — formal
    — general
    — off the job
    — future 'succession planning'
    — mechanics
    — one off experiences
- Flavour of the month
- Owned by personnel

doing already, rather than trying to put in a logical process of thoughtful analysis which they see as separate and not much to do with their real priorities.

Our director research enabled us to compare what the organization was trying to do with what it was perceived as achieving by those involved. I then compared the results of our research with the considerable literature on management development, and of course also related it to my own detailed working experience in half a dozen different organizations. The result of all this was the two charts in Figures 2.6 and 2.7. I use these charts as a way of getting people to review their own organizations. You may like to undertake the exercise for yourself.

Exercise

1   Consider each of the criteria in the two charts. Assess your own organization, in terms of how strongly you feel the criterion applies to it, on a scale 0 = low, 10 = high.

2   What are the reasons for any very high or very low scores on each of these charts? (Remember that the meaning of high or low is reversed, since a high score on a lever for success means that you believe you will be doing well, whereas a high score on the cause of failure suggests you will not be doing so well.)

When you have carried out this review yourself, you may like to consider using it with a wider audience: you can give it to your chief executive or to your management development committee if you have one. Perhaps you will just want to use it with colleagues either in the personnel department or in line management. One of the most valuable potential results of having a variety of people fill it in is to see the kind of differences which emerge. I had a very interesting experience of exactly this kind where the chief executive's view was different from the general view of several line managers; both sets of views again differed in some significant respects from the personnel director's views.

It may be worth re-emphasizing that the validity of the criteria suggested in these figures is something which you have to determine for yourself. The intentions and objectives of your scheme, as I said in the first paragraph in this section, may make some of the criteria irrelevant from your point of view. These irrelevant criteria can, however, stimulate, both in your mind and in the mind of others who may complete the exercise above, a useful discussion on exactly what kind of management development you are pursuing.

Charles Margerison[7] offers two lists indicating ways of achieving success in management development. He does not present them as a model, but it is convenient and appropriate to consider them here.

ACHIEVING SUCCESS IN MANAGEMENT DEVELOPMENT

Success

Success can be facilitated by:

- selecting high-achieving managers
- enthusiastic managerial support
- involving key people in diagnosing management development needs
- designing active work-related activities
- pressing hard for outputs
- providing early leadership experience
- letting each person appraise himself
- following up with workshops
- making line managers be accountable for management development

Failure

Failure is likely to arise when:

- there is no clear policy
- there is no top management support
- management development is not related to business plans
- there are inadequate diagnosis and *ad hoc* solutions
- political issues are ignored
- pay/promotion is unfair
- line support is low
- the buck is passed to the training department
- people are kept in jobs too long
- there is no regular follow up

Here again you can conduct a similar exercise for yourself on your view, and others' views, of management development in your own organization. In fact, you can use the same process of marking and involvement of others suggested for the earlier exercise.

One of the interesting differences between my lists and Margerison's is that he has included lack of top management support as a cause of failure. While such support is undoubtedly desirable, my research and experience show that it is not, in fact, an absolute requirement. I have encountered organizations where management development has proceeded very satisfactorily despite the fact that the chief executive and several of his main board colleagues were known to be uninterested. However, absence of top level support is an undeniable constraint and a limitation on what can be achieved. If management development is generally a failure it will be because there is no significant managerial support at any level.

BURGOYNE'S MODEL

Burgoyne[8] has made one of the few attempts to produce an explicit model of management development (Figure 2.8). The model emerged from a reanalysis of fourteen years' pure and applied research and development work in the Centre for the Study of Management Learning at Lancaster University. It aims to show what is involved 'in becoming a mature organisation in terms of management development'.

Figure 2.8 Levels of Maturity of Organizational Management Development

1 *No systematic management development*	2 *Isolated tactical management development*	3 *Integrated and coordinated structural and development tactics*	4 *A management development strategy to implement corporate policy*	5 *Management development strategy input to corporate policy formation*	6 *Strategic development of the management of corporate policy*
No systematic or deliberate management development in structural or developmental sense, total reliance on natural, *laissez-faire* uncontrived processes of management development	There are isolated and *ad hoc* tactical management development activities, of either structural or developmental kinds, or both, in response to local problems, crises, or sporadically identified general problems	The specific management development tactics which impinge directly on the individual manager, of career structure management, and of assisting learning, are integrated and coordinated	A management development strategy plays its part in implementing corporate policies through managerial human resource planning, and providing a strategic framework and direction for the tactics of career structure management and of learning, education and training	Management development processes feed information into corporate policy decision-making processes on the organization's managerial assets, strengths, weaknesses and potential and contribute to the forecasting and analysis of the manageability of proposed projects, ventures, changes	Management development processes enhance the nature and quality of corporate policy-forming processes, which they also inform and help implement

The first point to note is that Burgoyne defines management development as 'the management of managerial careers in an organisational context', and managerial careers as 'the biography of a person's managerial worklife'. He says that processes of 'natural' management development happen, they are not deliberately planned or contrived for management development. They are inevitable, usually good, and destined always to be the major provider of management development. However, in most situations he says they are not enough. In particular he sees these processes as essentially effective in new entrepreneurial firms, usually small in size. As such organizations need to cope with increasing scale and complexity, natural career structuring and learning alone are not sufficient, so the journey to what he calls 'organisational Management Development maturity' begins. As will be seen, all five levels of maturity after this first are variants of what I have called formal management development, Type 3.

In Burgoyne's view, possibly the majority of organizations are at levels 1 and 2. Levels 3 and 4 describe the limits of current best practice achieved 'with any consistency or thoroughness by what I would regard as the best organisations in these terms'. Levels 5 and 6 apparently exist as 'occasional achievements often precariously achieved and lost, and often only occurring in some relatively autonomous part of large organisations'.

Burgoyne has offered what seems to me a very recognizable and usable statement about the formal processes of management development. Understandably they follow from his definition of management development. Readers will have immediately noticed the difference of definition between us. The application of that difference can also be seen, in that what he describes as 'natural' management development processes and as 'usually good and destined always to be the major provider of management development', disappear from his model after level 1. It may be that he means to imply that such natural processes continue at all levels, but in fact no further attention is paid to them in the article. However, as a model of formal management development processes this seems to me an excellent formulation and one which could well be applied in reviewing your own position. You may wish to do so either in preference to the model I have suggested, because you wish to focus entirely on formal processes; or you may wish to use Burgoyne's model as an additional means of getting at the formal processes. Here is an exercise for you.

Exercise

1 Compare Burgoyne's definition of management development with Mumford's. Which do you propose to use in reviewing your own management development processes?
2 At what level of maturity do you believe your own organization to be, in terms of Burgoyne's model?
3 What steps would need to be taken by you, and by others, to move your organization upwards in terms of the levels described?

There is one other item not mentioned explicitly in my lists. One cause of failure can be that the whole process is driven by fads. Organizations get overwhelmed by the latest approach to appraisal, or decide to send all their top people to Harvard, or send everyone on an outdoor training course. My argument here would be that such fads emerge from more basic failures of the kind I have indicated. They arise when management development is not driven by business needs but by someone's idea of clever processes and when development activities are not appropriate either to need or to individuals.

Exercise

1 What model of Management Development have I been using so far?
2 Have my views been changed by reading this chapter?
3 What has been the model, or demonstrated beliefs and values, of my organization?
4 Is there a difference between our beliefs about management development and what we actually do and achieve? (One example would be a theoretical model which says managers are responsible for their own development, and a system which provides for all the initiatives to be taken by the organization and the managerial hierarchy.)
5 What conclusions do I draw from my answers to these questions? What actions should I, and what actions could I undertake as a result?

REFERENCES

1 STEWART R. *Choices for the manager*. McGraw Hill, 1982
2 MINTZBERG H. *The nature of managerial work*. Prentice-Hall, 1973
3 KOTTER J. P. *The general manager*. Macmillan, 1982
4 KOLB D. *Experiential learning*. Prentice-Hall, 1983
5 HONEY P. and MUMFORD A. *Manual of learning styles*. 3rd ed. Honey, 1992
6 REVANS R. W. *Action learning*. Blond and Briggs, 1980
7 MARGERISON C. 'Delivering success in management development'. *Journal of Management Development*. Vol 3, 1982
8 BURGOYNE J. 'Management development for the individual and the organisation'. *Personnel Management*. June 1988

3 Informal Management Development

THE CASE FOR INFORMAL DEVELOPMENT

In Chapter 1 the frequency and impact of informal learning experiences were identified by inviting readers to think about their own personal experiences and then to consider the position elsewhere in their organizations. Chapter 2 gave the reasons why so much managerial learning is unplanned and unstructured – though often very powerful: this is the nature of managerial work. Informal managerial learning is a byproduct of the variety of managerial tasks, the dynamic nature of managerial priorities, changes in the working environment, changes in colleagues and bosses, which all provide new opportunities and stimuli. So the clearest reason for including informal processes in our definition and models of management development is that excluding them takes us away from reality and eliminates from conscious consideration a number of potential opportunities for learning. This chapter shows how to improve those informal processes.

Informal learning is often seen by managers themselves as actually preferable to various forms of planned management development. Even if individuals work in organizations which have attempted various kinds of formal management development, they often none the less rate their informal experiences as much more significant.

Since at least the mid-1960s, with the push given to management education in the UK by the launch of the first major business schools and by the existence of Industrial Training Boards, attempts have been made to emphasize the importance of formal management development. Yet the reports by Professor Charles Handy[1] and Professor John Constable[2] have again made the point that there is insufficient formal provision for the development of managers. In terms of needs as expressed by these latter reports, and by comparative judgements against the development of managers in other countries (Handy), insufficient is done. The research of Professor Mangham, looking at the management training component, further supports that view.[3] That reseach, and Mangham's subsequent contribution to the Constable Report, shows that the majority of British managers receive no formal management training at all and that 20 per cent of companies employing more than 1,000 people had no provision for training their managers in 1985. Not surprisingly, the average for all managers is one day's training per year. No equivalent figure is available for the totality of formal management development, describing the extent to which other aspects such as planned personal development, job rotation or career planning are offered by organizations. It is probable that the figure for 'no action' organizations is higher. There are organizations which make use of courses in an unplanned way, but which lack any overall development scheme.

Particularly as far as courses are concerned, there are clear reasons why managers often find informal processes more effective than formal ones. These are:

- the content of development programmes, especially courses, which is experienced as unreal, irrelevant to the manager's priorities, or difficult to transfer from a course to a managerial job
- processes of learning which too often reflect the interests of course designers and tutors rather than managers
- processes which do not take into account different individual learning preferences

When I make the point to personnel directors and management development advisers that formal management development processes are often less effective than their providers perceive them to be, it is understandable that some of them seek to show that my evidence is flawed. The most frequently offered comment is that it is inevitable that managers will downgrade the importance of planned processes because they are unwilling to present themselves as needing to learn. The problem with accepting this defence is why it should apply to, for example, courses but not to other kinds of learning experience. Managers who said they had learned little of significance from courses were quite prepared to illustrate learning from informal processes. It is not at all clear why a manager's ego should prevent him from saying he has learned from a course but does not prevent him from saying that he has learned from a colleague, from a boss – or even from a subordinate!

The conclusion is not that formal management development should not be attempted, but rather that it should be improved. Chapters 4 to 8 set out ways of doing this. However, in terms of the balance of effort in management development, it would surely be sensible to pay attention to the messages which have now been sent to us for many years by managers themselves. In addition to whatever we should do to improve formal processes, we need to help managers to identify and make more effective use of the informal experiences which they so often highlight.

EXAMPLES OF INFORMAL ACCIDENTAL LEARNING

Problem Solving

I was a shift manager on a new production line in our plant. The line involved quite a bit of new technology and we had a number of problems with it. My immediate boss was a very ingenious guy with an engineering background. Every problem that came up he seemed to have an answer for, but the problems kept coming up. His boss the Production Director called all three shift managers and our boss to his office. He had two flip charts; one he marked 'Problems', the other he divided into two columns: 'Causes apparent' and 'Causes deeper?' After forty minutes with him we did not come out with a single answer, whereas five minutes with our boss always produced an answer. The difference was we came out with the questions we needed to pursue in order to produce really effective answers. I learned two things – one was about looking deeper into problems, and the other was about how to make the best use of the intelligence of five people working together.

Project

Our research people came up with a major technological breakthrough. The issue was to convert it into several products, and to get them on to the market before any of our competitors found out what we were doing. I was put in charge of the whole exercise – production, finance, marketing. My company had never tried a really integrated approach to managing the introduction of new products before. All the barons had looked after their own territory, which meant all the decisions got pushed up to the Management Committee. As a result it was assumed that everybody had to fight for their own resources, argue with each other about the best way to do things, and particularly to make sure that the other guy got blamed when things went wrong. I showed it could be done differently and better. I suppose that was learning both for me and for the organization.

Presentation

I had always thought I was pretty good at putting my ideas over. Right from university days I found I could argue clearly but pleasantly, and influence people. I had found the same in my early years in management in business. Most people were so relieved to find someone who could put over an idea clearly in a few sentences instead of in pages that I got quite a reputation for it. Then I was moved from my then department to an area I did not know very well. I was faced with having to make a presentation to a visiting American director. I got my new subordinates to brief me beforehand and then I launched into presentation with some nice slides, some good specifics and a few jokes. I was absolutely self-confident about it. I was jabbed to death by the Director – he wanted to know a lot more than I knew. We went off to lunch and when I saw him coming towards me I thought I was in for another going over. I was astonished when he told me that my summary at the beginning was excellent. Then he added the comment which really reinforced what I had gone through. 'It is practically never worthwhile pretending you know more than you do.' Experience has since confirmed what I learned that day.

Redundancy

We had to make some supervisors redundant. I should think we made every mistake in the book. We did not have individual packages properly prepared. We actually allowed rumours to go out beforehand, because we thought it would soften the blow. We saw them first thing in the morning and then let them stay on the plant, instead of telling them in mid-afternoon and sending them home. We made a lot of mistakes including now I think of it the fairly basic one of not finding out what other people's experience was. It was awful. But we did do it better next time.

Selling

We had built our company from selling professional services on a day rate basis. We managed to negotiate contracts so that there was no prior agreement on the total that would be involved in any project. The basis for this was that neither we nor the client usually knew what the total cost could be, even in terms of likely numbers of days. Then we were faced with a really major project, for a client who wanted to change the basis of the contract to a fixed price. The project and the client both were great opportunities for us. But actually negotiating on a quite different basis really stretched us. The real problem was not negotiation skills. It was understanding the different objectives and priorities of the client. It took us a long time to understand why they wanted it differently. It was a basic selling message really. The customer is always right, but we wasted a lot of time trying to persuade him he was wrong.

Committee Meeting

I attended a meeting with my boss and five other colleagues at the same level as myself. It was our formal annual review with his boss, and his staff supports. My boss was shown up in the worst way. What his boss did was to get the rest of us to challenge each other's budgets and priorities. He really worked on us, and pushed our boss to one side. I think all of us lost in that situation. Although we didn't recognize it at the time, I think the five of us lost out because it was clear we were not a team. Our boss lost out because his boss put him down. I expect the top guy thought he was the winner, but he was not really. None of us respected him for what he had done, because we saw what kind of game he was playing.

Business Visit

We acquired a new company in the United States. I was sent over with a colleague with a brief that we should look at some issues about how they managed their business, what sort of controls they used and what sort of review processes. There were actually some useful things I learned there in terms of the different ways in which they did things. Looking back on it however I can see I learned some more subtle things as well. As much as anything else the differences were about what you saw the job of managers to be and how they behaved in a company which had great similarities to our own, and in which the only major difference was that they were American.

Observing

I was made assistant to a manager who was temporarily running two different jobs. They just threw me at him as a bright young resource, who might be able to help him. He was so busy that he could never sit down with me to sort out what he wanted me to do. So a lot of the time I was underemployed. I volunteered to go round with him and make notes at meetings he had, and particularly to go with him on some visits he had to make to some old customers. I certainly did give him some useful notes, but I made a hell of a lot more which I kept for myself. The main thing I learned was the obvious, that if you want to manage your time better, you have to invest some time to do it – he never did. Otherwise I learned a lot of things actually about his skills in particular situations. He was extraordinarily good at not only listening but showing that he was listening. His whole body leaned towards the speaker, and on top of that he would summarize what the other chap had said – often actually expressing his view better than it had been delivered.

WHAT THESE EXAMPLES MEAN

These examples are the tip of an iceberg – in two senses. First, they are a tiny proportion of the full range of incidents from managerial work that provide learning experiences. Second, they are the tip of an iceberg for any particular individual. In both senses there are far more examples than are:

- identified in general as possible opportunities for learning
- identified, used and reviewed as learning experiences by any individual

So we return to one of our early propositions. Informal, accidental experiences are widely present but often badly identified and in consequence inefficiently used. When managers are asked to review their stimulating learning experiences they will often quote cases like those just given. However, many of them also recognize that they did not make the most of these experiences or even recognize them unassisted. The best of all possible news is precisely that managers do recognize that these often powerfully experienced managerial processes are also learning experiences, *but that as learning experiences they could be improved*, with significant benefit to themselves and their organization.

It is sensible to answer some of the questions which may arise, particularly with people who see the concept of management development as being about formal processes. Learning from experience, although ever present, is for many purposes not only inefficient but insufficient. It is just possible that managers, if not management development advisers, will become so excited by the possibilities which follow in the next section that they will decide that formal management development processes are really quite unnecessary. Since this book is promoting the idea of a balance, using both informal and formal, I would clearly not subscribe to abandoning formal processes. There are some very major deficiencies in a total reliance on informal processes.

They include:

- *Idealization* – attitudes and behaviours which say that past experience is so valued and appropriate that it is all that is necessary. Effective learning involves building successfully on properly understood past experience, not treating it as the only process of merit.
- *Narrowness* – it is possible for a manager's work experience to be extremely narrow in terms of jobs, functions, kinds of organization and sizes of organization. While effective management development is more likely to focus on the specific than the general, this does not mean that a manager in retail needs to know nothing about, for instance, production processes.
- *Obsolescence* – painful and perhaps carefully acquired experience of how to do a managerial job may well become out of date. The appropriate attitudes and behaviour of managers in public service utilities who change to meet the new demands of privatized business are a case in point. As a director said rather ruefully, 'I reached the top of this organization by being better than most at managing a centralized bureaucratic business. Now I am here, I have to manage newly created profit centres with managers who want a decision yesterday.' If you learn only from what you encounter in the normal and natural processes of work at a particular level, this may mean that you will not be exposed to those activities or opportunities which you will actually need in future.
- In addition to the particular nature of the organization, there is the specific issue of the closest relationship of all, with bosses and colleagues. These may be excellent providers of advice and good models of effective behaviour – or they may be neither.
- Of course people develop skills from the 'natural' process of doing the job, and finding out whether the way they do it works. If it does they understandably assume that they have a skill. However, the skill they have acquired may be either

inappropriate or at an insufficiently high performance level. At worst it may even be the wrong kind of skill. One example is the process of interviewing. The skills which many managers deploy in selection interviewing have been acquired from the experience of being interviewed themselves, and then of interviewing others. Their level of skill is often, however, well below what they need to interview effectively.

DEVELOPING TYPE 2 LEARNING

Type 2 learning is defined as the process of integrating learning and managerial work, so that both are given conscious attention. The best way to test the proposition, and then to show how normal managerial work can be used more effectively for learning purposes, is to start with the following exercise.

Exercise

1 Look back over your last four weeks of managerial work. Pick out the most crucial, highest priority, the most significant things with which you have been involved.
2 What results were achieved from the managerial work (by you or someone else)?
3 Have you learned something from the results achieved, and/or from the process by which the results were achieved?

It will be noted that, in contrast to the learning biography exercise with which we started in Chapter 1, we start here with managerial activity rather than learning experience. There are several reasons for this. The first is that in my experience of using both these exercises, some managers have problems with the first, but very few with the second. On the first exercise, where we ask managers to identify significant learning experiences, some people have difficulty recognizing a 'learning experience', and have to be helped with lists of possible opportunities – as indeed the reader may have found in Chapter 1. But managers do not have problems in thinking about managerial activities. Nor do they usually have much problem in identifying some achieved learning from at least one of these over a four-week period, though some of them do say in tones of surprise, 'So that's what you mean by learning'.

The other major reason for starting with managerial activities when we are trying to help people achieve Type 2 experiences is that we are actually proposing that they should work in that way in their real-life situation. We are not asking them to think about learning opportunities first, and then to work out how their managerial activities might be used or tailored to meet the learning need. Appropriate as this process can be, this is a Type 3 kind of process, where the development of the manager is the initiating and perhaps prime concern.

At this point the reader may be saying 'But aren't you talking about exactly the same kind of experience? For example, you quoted a project experience as a Type 1 case earlier on, yet in my organization we use projects very much as development tools – what you would call Type 3.' The need to answer this question, and the use of the project as an illustration, brings out a very important point. Management development advisers very often see projects as useful vehicles for development, most particularly in the action learning process. However, the main interest and focus of most managers, *even in a formal development process*, is usually to complete the project itself successfully, providing it is realistic and has not been invented simply for development purposes. The great virtue of projects within the action learning process is that they provide a balance between managerial work and learning from the managerial work. In terms of our clarification of Type 2, however, the crucial point is that here we are using a project as a Type 2 example where the initiating force for the project is the line manager, not the person responsible for management development. The development programme may have a very careful and sophisti-cated process for choosing projects which are realistic in terms of commitment and felt accountability, and indeed fundamental, to the development of the organization. However, the great difference from the projects which managers talk about as learning experiences is that they start from outside the normal managerial process. The great virtue of an exercise like this is that it starts from where managers are, rather than requiring an understanding about a different kind of process called 'learning'.

The second feature of the exercise – aside from its reality and the fact that it takes us straight into what we mean by Type 2 learning – is that it brings out a process which Peter Honey and I call 'retrospective learning'. Informal accidental managerial learning is usually only partially understood and recognized when it happens. It is also, by our definition, wholly unplanned. All the examples given earlier in this chapter were of unplanned accidental learning – Type 1. They became a form of retrospective learning simply because the managers who described them were recalling particular experiences and reviewing them for me. The wording of many of the narratives makes it clear that it was precisely the process of description and review that identified the learning experience as such. This process not only identified the fact of learning, but in many cases clarified what the learning had actually been. The managers involved recognized more clearly:

- what they had learned
- (in some cases) produced a deeper analysis of what they had learned
- (in some cases) increased their understanding of how they had learned

As with many other managerial activities, it is the provision of an opportunity to stand back mentally, review and analyse the results of the review, which produces a useful result. And again, it is precisely the absence of the process of reviewing, rather than its presence, which is the norm.

So the first stage in any attempt to encourage Type 2 learning is to facilitate retrospective learning. This is the easiest thing for managers to grasp; it is very productive in terms of immediately accessible examples from their own experience, and does not involve the kind of hypothetical constructions about future activities which many of them initially find difficult.

The next stage, still concentrating on the retrospective process, may well be to widen managers' vision about the kind of activities which may have provided opportunities for learning. You may have already made use of the learning opportunities chart (Figure 1.2). If you have not done so, or you want to try this out with some managers, you could do the following exercise:

Exercise

1 Consider the list of learning opportunities. Have any of these been particularly important to you in your present job/in a past job?
2 Consider whether you learned something significant from one of these activities.
3 Consider why you learned.
4 Consider how you learned.

There are a number of things which can be done either as exercises in the form just indicated, or simply with questions posed during relevant discussions with managers, which can bring them into a discussion of how they have *actually* learned from past experience.

The other major element in Type 2 managerial learning is to move to the more difficult but very productive stage of 'prospective learning'. One of the great advantages of a considered discussion of retrospective learning is that it does not have to be left as a purely evocative review, collecting with hindsight useful information from the past. It can be linked to prospective learning simply by asking managers who have identified useful retrospective experiences whether they can see any similar or indeed different learning opportunities which may arise in the future. Again our emphasis in Type 2 is to deal with such opportunities primarily as managerial activities, not learning opportunities. The exercise is:

Can you think of some similar or different managerial activities with which you are going to be involved over say the next three or four weeks, from which you might think to acquire some new knowledge or understanding, or you might test out a skill?

The final stage in developing prospective learning opportunities is to build on any success you or others have had in identifying the opportunities. Simply recognizing in advance that something represents an opportunity is better than not thinking about it at all. However, you can benefit even more from planning in a little more detail what your learning objectives will be and how you propose to set about taking advantage of the opportunity. This is admittedly the most difficult of the suggestions made so far. It may well be appropriate for many managers to stay, at least initially, at the level of identifying the opportunity, without being pressed too hard to develop plans on how to take full advantage of it.

A manager who has identified a prospective learning opportunity should subsequently review the extent to which he or she has taken advantage of it. (This incidentally brings us on to one of the issues that often arises with the kind of personal development plans which managers can adopt in a fit of enthusiasm at the end of a course. There is no process for reviewing the success or otherwise of the plan, and since it is often divorced from normal managerial activity it tends to stay in the development file after the Type 3 event which has created it.) Since in Type 2 we are always working on real managerial activities, the likelihood that the prospective learning opportunity will be lost is reduced. It may disappear because the activity disappears; but so long as the activity actually happens there is a greater likelihood of both the activity and its derived learning opportunity being reviewed.

The retrospective and prospective learning approaches are illustrated in Figure 3.1. In many ways it would be useful to adopt

Figure 3.1 Retrospective and Prospective Learning

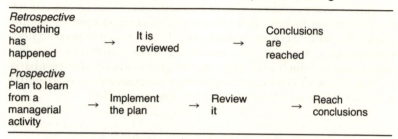

an alternative design for the prospective learning opportunity. We could make use of a concept initially developed, for slightly different reasons, by Professor John Morris, who used a learning spiral rather than a learning circle. The idea is that retrospective learning experiences lead to the identification of prospective opportunities, which in turn lead to retrospective learning which in turn lead to . . . Chapter 11 provides a further breakdown of different approaches to learning, introducing the idea of the intuitive and incidental approaches. We have emphasized retrospective and prospective approaches here because of their greater productivity in learning terms. The reader may ask at this point why I have provided such detailed exercises rather than simply explaining the nature of Type 2 development and then providing a list of examples. The reader has been taken through the process of actually carrying out the exercise because the process is more likely to be understood and accepted if an individual has carried it out personally. The detailed working through of the exercises is necessary to secure understanding of an unfamiliar process. In terms of learning, it is more effective to involve the reader in actively doing something rather than passively looking at an interesting list of opportunities.

QUALITY IN RETROSPECTIVE LEARNING

The first series of examples I gave were Type 1, because they were unplanned and the manager involved did not consciously identify them as learning experiences. They illustrate what can be achieved in Type 2 because they were subsequently reviewed with me by the participant manager. Without such a discussion and review they would have remained disorganized, fragmentary and only partially remembered. Even a relatively short discussion with someone else can add depth and understanding to achieved learning; it is this which turns a Type 1 experience into a Type 2.

However, this is still a fairly low level Type 2 experience. The list of examples is accidental and informal in origin, and the discussion about them was accidental too – it so happened that I came along and acquired managers' statements (not always in the context of me trying to find out what managers had learned – sometimes simply through a discussion of other managerial problems and processes). The essential quality of the Type 2 experience really resides in the care and thought that go into it. As shown earlier, this can be entirely dedicated to a good retrospective review or to a good analysis of prospective experiences. The main point is that experiences should cease to be seen as exclusively managerial with some fringe learning tacked on. They are managerial activities from which some deliberate learning is derived through conscious thought and discussion.

Lee Iacocca's original book[4] provides a number of excellent illustrations of how he applied things he had learned at Ford to his new situation at Chrysler. The descriptions of how he learned from his Ford experiences – partly by observing the failures of others – what he should do as the new boss in Chrysler – for example ensuring that he was not the only new man when he went there – are important, high level illustrations. However it is given to few of us to move from being one of the three most powerful people in Ford to becoming the most powerful person in Chrysler.

Here is another example, this time about a young manager in his late 20s. He describes one of the people he had worked for:

> He would take time in joint problem solving to let me reach my own conclusions, coaching me as necessary through my thinking processes. Sometimes this led to outcomes which he probably anticipated. On other occasions an unexpected solution emerged and he would say 'That's interesting' and be prepared to develop it. He worked hard at problem solving and thinking laterally, and coached me in the techniques he favoured.
>
> His coaching and encouragement extended beyond the immediate problem. He helped me use the organiz-

ation's political system to get scarce resources and prompted me to improve presentations.

Here we begin to face one of the associated issues. Whereas a great deal of Type 1 learning is entirely solitary and is appreciated only by the individual who claims the learning, Type 2 is much more likely to involve other people, 'Involve' means that the learning is placed on the table between at least two participants, probably a manager and the boss in most situations, or perhaps between a manager and one or more colleagues. Discussion of both options, prospective learning and achieved learning (retrospective learning), are likely to be enhanced by checking them out with other people. It is partly through this process of openness, sharing and to at least some extent, partnership, that some of the weaknesses of learning from experience are reduced. It is much easier to remain in a self-satisfied cocoon about your achieved learning and performance if you keep your views of both to yourself. If you have to, or decide to, check them out with someone else then you are quite likely to get some information which confirms your view and some which challenges it.

This takes us into organizational learning, the process by which an organization changes its nature, culture and direction. In another sense it takes us into the field of Chris Argyris, of double loop learning, where received wisdom is challenged. Argyris[5] discusses some of the issues involved here, and in particular explains how the processes of single loop learning and the correction of errors in itself militates against double loop learning, where values and beliefs are actually challenged.

WHO CAN HELP?

The chart which follows (Figure 3.2) indicates that there are essentially five types of people who can help an individual improve learning on the job. Since each of them can help him in both Type

Figure 3.2   Helpers with Type 2 Processes

Boss
Mentor
Peers
Subordinates
Network contacts

2 and Type 3 learning situations, I have drawn both processes together in Chapter 9 and will not duplicate the details here.

The main point here is to distinguish between the kind of initiative which may be taken. A boss or a mentor is more likely to take the initiative in discussing Type 2 experiences with a manager. Colleagues are likely to do so only at the initiative of another manager seeking help or because they themselves want help on one of their own learning opportunities. Subordinates are, of course, extremely unlikely to take the initiative in setting up a Type 2 learning experience from their boss; however, they can be very useful in providing feedback about particular experiences, observations of what has happened at meetings and, if the relationship is particularly good, they may even offer comments about their boss's performance.

It will be noted that the personnel director or management development advisers do not appear. There is a paradox here. All the suggestions in this chapter are in the first place directed at exactly these people. Why then are they not shown as helpers? Because the Type 2 context is one owned by managers and their colleagues. We want them to identify their own opportunities from their own activities and their own experiences. The roles of personnel and management development advisers are entirely subsidiary. They may help to the extent of some informal discussions, perhaps offering some of the exercises indicated in this chapter. They might choose to help in a much more serious way through the various opportunities existing in the current formal management development processes. In this case we should finish with the irony that Type 2 processes may be stimulated by discussion of Type 3 processes. However, the ways in which that can be done will be left to the chapters where we talk about Type 3 processes, and to Chapter 9.

HOW DOES A MANAGER START?

The manager creates Type 2 learning experiences by thinking about and reviewing normal managerial activities. These can be identified purely 'in the head'. Alternatively, they can be found by a review of various kind of (mainly written) material:

- *a review of priorities and objectives*, which may indicate areas of significance or novelty

- *a job description* (if the manager has gone into a new job or responsibilities have recently been changed)
- *an activity list* of the kind many managers keep as a daily or weekly reminder of things to do, or a note on actions which have been set up and need to be followed through
- *a work diary* which may simply indicate some of the most important events on a daily basis, which again may highlight interesting activities either already undertaken or to be undertaken
- *a development plan*, perhaps produced through some Type 3 process such as appraisal or a course
- *a learning log*, where a manager deliberately keeps a review of learning experiences and opportunities
- *discussion with colleagues*, where one or more colleagues identify similar activities and experiences which may provide learning
- *individual discussion with boss*, where some specific activity is related to a learning opportunity
- *a Type 2 learning review* of the kind illustrated in this chapter

Further discussion on how to create Type 2 learning is given in Chapter 9, and detailed guidance is provided in various books and articles.[6]

WHAT STIMULATES LEARNING ON THE JOB?

Some of the things which bring about individual learning are recognizable in the case studies quoted in this chapter. Davies and Easterby-Smith[7] say, as a result of their research, that

> managers develop primarily through confrontations with novel situations and problems where their existing repertoire of behaviours are inadequate and where they have to develop new ways of dealing with these situations. In general it is unlikely that there will be any shortage of novel situations facing organisations in the future.

This statement is a little too strong; it depends what you mean by 'novel'. Many of the examples encountered in my own research would not fit a definition of 'novel' if this implied something totally new and different. However, the pressure for change, whether it is within an existing job or caused by taking up a new one, certainly forces recognition of both the need to learn and the occasion of learning. (See Chapter 11 for further discussion.)

The process of taking up a new job necessarily involves a degree of novelty and different stages and pressures of learning. These are well described by Gabarro.[8] My own view of the implications of job changes is shown in Figure 3.3.

Figure 3.3 Learning Problems in Job Moves

Familiar	Same function, same organization
Part familiar	Same function, different organization
	Different function, same organization
Unfamiliar	New job, new organization

A second pressure to learn on the job is the recognition of significant problems in relationships or performance. These may be indicated through a formal Type 3 process, but they are more often indicated by informal processes – unsuccessful attempts to influence others, a failure of others to respond to your initiatives or a failure to meet managerial targets. These kind of occasions can be variously described as a jolt, or as stronger psychological disturbances of pain or shock. A number of these are described in an interesting article by Snell[9] who has also described how to try and reduce the pain or discomfort. Kelleher *et al.*,[10] in a somewhat confusing article, identify three factors in the work context. These are:

* freedom – the extent to which managers' activity contained opportunities for self-initiative
* support, including issues such as how far rewards, communication and feedback encourage learning
* structure – boundaries, limits and constraints which channel managerial effort and energy

Stuart[11] brings out a very important point about language. He compares formal methods of training with everyday forms of managerial behaviour. He compares the formal case study with the everyday form 'You'll never guess what's happened to me. There I was, and she said: What would you have done?' Stuart is bringing out the important point that natural descriptions of normal behaviour are recognizable and acceptable to managers. By implication, the processes described in this chapter will be attractive precisely because they build on the kind of natural language he describes.

Exercise

1 How might I set about improving informal learning processes in my organization?
2 Can I make use of the ideas of converting Type 1 to Type 2 managerial experiences?
3 Can I identify some good retrospective and perhaps even some good prospective learners in my organization?
4 How might I use these individuals to help others to learn more effectively from informal processes?

REFERENCES

1 HANDY C. *The making of managers*. NEDO, 1987
2 CONSTABLE J. *The making of British managers*. BIM/NEDO, 1987
3 MANGHAM I. *Management training*. University of Bath, 1986
4 IACOCCA L. *Iacocca*. Sidgwick and Jackson, 1985
5 ARGYRIS C. *Reasoning learning and action*. Jossey Bass, 1982
6 MUMFORD A. *Developing top managers*. Gower, 1988; MUMFORD A., HONEY P. and ROBINSON G. *Developing directors: making experience count*, IOD, 1990; and HONEY P. and MUMFORD A. *Manual of learning opportunities*. Honey, 1989
7 DAVIES J. and EASTERBY-SMITH M. 'Learning and developing from managerial work experiences'. *Journal of Management Studies*. Vol 21, No 4, 1984
8 GABARRO J. 'When a new manager takes charge'. *Harvard Business Review*. May–June 1985
9 SNELL R. 'The emotional cost of learning at work'. *Management Education and Development*. Vol 19, Pt 4, 1988
10 KELLEHER D., FINESTONE P. and LOWRY A. 'Managerial learning: first notes from an unstudied frontier'. *Organizational Studies*. Vol 11, No 3, 1986
11 STUART R. 'Towards reestablishing naturalism in management training and development'. *Industrial and Commercial Training*. July 1984

4 Systems for Development – Appraisal

The number of books and articles on this subject shows how crucial it is in the formal system (see Further Reading). In many ways it is the Holy Grail of management development. In principle it deals with one of the major issues about improving performance; yet the practice is often profoundly unsatisfactory. The most useful guide is Randell *et al.*[1]

THE STARTING POINT – THE JOB ITSELF

Planned development ought to be based on a clear, formal view of the content of the manager's job. At an individual level this means that there ought to be a job description and some statement of priorities, preferably drawn up on a three- to twelve-month cycle. To attempt to develop managers for jobs whose purpose and nature are unclear, where the constraints and opportunties are unspecified, and where the boundaries are undefined, is to risk losing both sharpness and commitment to any subsequent development process. Chapter 2 touched on the contingent nature of managerial work, and this is expanded in Chapter 6. The idea that 'everyone knows what managers need to be able to do', and the consequent argument 'all managers ought to be exposed to . . .' is likely to be a cause of failure in formal development processes. The particular skills or competences required are covered in Chapter 6.

   Clarity of job purpose and clarity about priorities would themselves be a considerable step forward in many organizations. They would help to at least address the issue of what kind of problems and circumstances the manager needs to be able to overcome and what the purpose of development activities might be.

This basic level of understanding is usefully supplemented in some organization by further clarification. A list of priorities agreed on an informal basis, with perhaps only a note exchanged between boss and subordinate afterwards, can be extended. There might be a list of key result areas, or a formal process for agreeing objectives and priorities as part of a structured management system. Historically the management-by-objectives approach was introduced in part through management development schemes and to satisfy management development needs as much as management systems needs; this is still the case in some organizations.

In other organizations job clarification may extend to a much more detailed statement like the Hay job description process, which clearly draws out the issue of accountability. This can be very helpful not only for analysing the job itself, but for clarifying aspects of the job for current development (although not for future development needs).

APPRAISAL AND PERFORMANCE REVIEW

This chapter deals with the *purpose* of reviewing individual performance and the problems that arise from attempting to do so. The *consequence* of the review is covered in Chapter 6.

A survey carried out in 1986 showed that 82 per cent of employers operate performance appraisal schemes.[2] It is not only small companies that do not use such schemes: public and local government organizations are less likely to have such schemes than commercial organizations of comparable size. But any organization with formal management development, or proposing to develop it in the future, is likely to go in for some form of performance appraisal. The problems of appraisal have been consistent, and were already visible twenty-five years ago in the work of McGregor, Drucker and Rowe. What we have had since is a constant rediscovery that *in principle* performance appraisal meets a genuine need both of individual managers in their real work processes and of a formal management development scheme. We know that it is frequently attempted, that organizations constantly rediscover familiar difficulties and that appraisal schemes are often perceived by managers as ineffective. We will now look at the main issues.

Objectives

Research on appraisal schemes, and general experience, shows that many of the problems in conducting effective appraisal start with confusion over objectives. The confusion may arise because the scheme may not make clear what the objectives are. Alternatively, an appraisal scheme may be designed to have a number of objectives – explicit or not – which in practice turn out to conflict with each other. Possible objectives for an appraisal scheme include:

- providing information for succession and resource planning
- providing a basis for improved communication between boss and subordinate
- identifying and recording performance weaknesses
- providing a basis for analysis of performance and identification of required standards and improvements
- identifying potential
- providing mutual feedback between boss and subordinate
- providing a basis for training and career counselling
- providing a basis for salary decision making.

It is theoretically unlikely, and certainly so in practice, that a single appraisal scheme will meet all of these diverse objectives. Perhaps more important is the fact that some of the objectives actually conflict with each other. The most familiar instance is that appraisal related to salary decisions is generally found to be ineffective at providing realistic performance-improvement discussion or improved feedback between boss and subordinate. None the less, Long's survey[2] reported that 40 per cent of companies associate their appraisals with salary decisions.

Methods of Appraisal

Obviously enough, the methods chosen for an appraisal scheme or for individual appraisal discussions ought to relate to the objectives which have been set. An open, frank and free exchange about problems in performance is more feasible, and more likely to be attained, if the objectives are to improve immediate feedback between boss and subordinate and to identify performance issues relevant to both of them. If the appraisal is to be used for succession planning or salary determination, open, frank and free exchange is likely to be inhibited.

Similarly, the extent to which the subordinate is asked to contribute to the appraisal, perhaps through conducting a self-appraisal, is also influenced both in prospect and in actuality by the subordinate's knowledge of how the information will be used.

Recognition of Benefits

The major advantage of appraisal is that people like to know what is expected of them, how they are measured and what their boss thinks of their performance. The normal day-to-day processes of managerial relationships do not satisfy these needs. Too often, however, appraisal schemes pursue sophisticated objectives but fail to meet basic needs.

For appraisal to be effective and useful at any level other than that of recording words for longer-range salary or succession planning issues, those who conduct and participate in it must both see some positive benefits for themselves. All too often neither boss nor subordinate actually recognizes such benefits. Bosses do not always recognize that benefits which may exist for them do not exist for their subordinates; equally, bosses and subordinates tend to have different perceptions about the potential benefits to each other.

Ownership

The question of who owns the appraisal scheme is actually associated with the last point. Appraisal schemes tend to be introduced, sold and maintained by personnel people, and are not owned in any real sense by the line managers. Line managers particularly will not feel they own the scheme if they have had no say in determining either the principle or the detailed procedures involved. Since the process tends to be difficult and since the benefits tend not to be recognized by the individuals involved it is understandable that line managers lack commitment.

The problem of securing their commitment is that the process of consulting all those who might feel they have the right to contribute to decisions on both principle and method is extremely time consuming, and tends to be seen as unnecessary by the top people in an organization who have been persuaded to accept appraisal. Desirable though it is to have such support at top level, this will not in itself secure involvement in the spirit of the appraisal system; it may simply lead to a grudging completion of forms rather than the genuine involvement which is necessary to achieve any of the potential objectives of appraisal.

This problem is particularly acute if the chosen objectives for appraisal include the identification of improved performance requirements and the improvement of feedback between boss and subordinate. These extremely difficult processes will not be undertaken successfully if bosses are 'doing' appraisal because they are required to rather than because they have been helped to see how it could benefit them.

Rewards

The perception of benefit by boss and subordinate, and preferably both, provides one kind of reward. If the boss believes that the appraisal process will actually help him secure more effective performance from an individual or department, then he will expect to receive a psychological reward. The reward may be positive – the feeling by himself or others that things are improving – or negative – the reduction of criticism and unpleasantness. The reward may be the purely personal one of having carried out a difficult managerial task well.

It is not easy to find examples of managers securing rewards from appraisal. In practice they get rewarded for their performance on issues usually seen as more directly relevant to managerial effectiveness. A manager may be lucky enough to have a boss who is interested in effective appraisal, but the organization usually provides only a negative reward – the absence of nagging from personnel for not having completed the forms (which of course have little to do with effective appraisal).

There is much more scope than is generally recognized for rewarding managers for undertaking, and doing a good job on, appraisal. At the least, they can be helped to see how they can get personal satisfaction out of doing it well. More ambitiously, the organization could develop the processes by which managers are given feedback on the quality and effectiveness of their appraisals.

Previous Experience

Appraisal schemes nowadays rarely spring up as totally new activities in a company; previous experience either within the organization or with previous employers will obviously affect the enthusiasm with which particular managers enter the scheme and influence the way they behave.

Managerial Style Requirements

One of the difficulties for many bosses is that effective appraisal for improvement and development purposes requires them to behave in a way foreign to their normal managerial style. They are required to be reflective and analytical; good listeners rather than authoritative, immediate decision takers leading a discussion. Not many managers have the flexibility to behave or, at least, to behave credibly in this way. They need to be helped to recognize the behaviour which particular appraisal objectives require them to adopt. Where they are unable to adapt their behaviour, they need help to deal with the consequences of that inability.

Wider Context

Although appraisal essentially has to do with the individual's contribution appraisal discussions seem too rarely to take note of the fact that the individual is performing within a particular context. The results achieved may have been achieved more or less easily depending on factors in the general environment: the difficulties of staffing within a department and difficulties of relationships with outside agencies or departments. The absence of this kind of consideration explains why appraisals of particular individuals tend to slide up and down a scale of perceived achievement because not enough weight has been placed on the factors which have affected either good or bad performance or achievement of particular results. Most important of all, of course, is the contribution of the boss to the subordinate's own performance. It would be an unusual manager who registered this on a subordinate's appraisal form, which is why many appraisal systems use the 'grandfather' to introduce that kind of comment, usually through a special section on the form.

Appraisal Bureaucracy and Appraisal Help

The comments above suggest that the help most appraisal schemes need from personnel is assistance in clarifying objectives and ensuring that the objectives chosen for an appraisal scheme are appropriate and valid. Individual managers also need help in dealing with particular appraisal circumstances. However, what most personnel departments provide is important but insufficient: persistence in the bureaucracy of appraisal through designing forms and monitoring how many of their staff particular managers have appraised.

Appraising Potential

Some management development schemes emphasize development for future rather than current jobs. The identification of potential is often the least satisfactory part of the appraisal system and can appear as a misplaced symbolic gesture rather than an effective management process. It might well be better to separate it from the normal review – but most organizations do not. A manager capable of helping to identify performance issues with his subordinates is not necessarily equally capable of identifying the same person's potential for other jobs in the organization, perhaps even for his own job. The discussion of potential and career planning between boss and subordinate has different psychological and control problems. A substantial section on potential and career planning follows in Chapter 5.

Drawing out Development Needs

It is also true that many managers find it difficult to switch from reviewing performance to talking about training and development; they give these issues far too little attention. It could therefore be sensible to separate them. Many firms do so on the form, but do not require that the discussion is held separately. It is difficult to get the manager to give time for both sets of review. There is a limit to the amount of time that a manager will spend on something which offers few rewards and has many difficulties.

Standards Used in Appraisal – Performance or Personality?

Many systems now concentrate on assessing against pre-agreed priorities or objectives or against the job description rather than against personality characteristics such as initiative, dependability or judgement. These characteristics are extremely difficult to define and measure.

Where appraisal schemes concentrate on results rather than characteristics some of the problems of different standards, halo or skew rating become less crucial. The review by Long[2] says that 63 per cent of forms deal with results, but that 29 per cent have rating of personality traits – some forms cover both.

Some people have experimented with generalized views of managerial skills like the Fayol headings of planning, organizing, motivating, leading and controlling. Although these appear better than the personality characteristics they are in practice very difficult to define in terms which are acceptable to both parties. Which two managers, for example, would agree on what is meant by being effective as a leader? The most difficult but the best approach is to identify the explicit managerial behaviour needed.

The Form

Some managers will say that the best form is a blank sheet of paper; others prefer lots of leading questions which help them to identify the course of the appraisal discussion. Standard forms tend to be required not for discussion and feedback between manager and subordinate, but for some other reason – usually to contribute to the organization's succession or resource plan.

THE SKILLS REQUIRED

The failure of some appraisal processes has clearly been due in some instances to the absence of the required skills. Many managers are simply not capable without formal training (and some not even then) of conducting appraisal in a way which satisfactorily meets even one of the potential objectives, let alone many. Their capacity to make accurate judgements or to listen or give feedback which can be heard and acted on is all too often lacking. Even when managers have learnt the theory of effective appraisal processes, including the skills of listening and effective feedback, applying the theory away from the training course or the guidance booklet often causes difficulties. A fascinating example of this is to be found in the x and y case discussed by Argyris.[3] His experience is that even people (including personnel specialists) who have defined the problems and established what behaviour is desirable in advance, will revert to precisely those behaviours which they know in principle are negative and ineffective when reviewing an ineffective subordinate in a formal training context.

INDIVIDUAL RESULTS FROM APPRAISAL

The extent to which this process actually improves performance, where that is one of the immediately desired outcomes, is more often demonstrated by anecdote than by research. The impact on the identification of appropriate development processes is often even more tenuous. This is in part because many appraisal forms have been designed with unhelpful headings or boxes in terms of identifying what those development needs and, more particularly, what the development solutions might be. Thus a form may include two very large but relatively empty boxes:

* What are the development needs?
* What solutions do you recommend?

Sometimes forms will include questions on whether a manager should attend a training course to remedy any weaknesses identified. When associated with the catalogue of training courses that some particularly large organizations produce, this kind of form design has the advantage of tending to produce more specific recommendations, but sometimes on a standardized basis not related to the real needs of different individuals.

Either as part of an assessment of potential, or perhaps more helpfully as part of the preparation of a general development programme, desirable job moves can sometimes be highlighted by the design of the form. This can be very helpful, providing again that it is related to the real needs of individuals rather than to some overgeneralized statement that all managers should be moved at intervals of 2.5 years.

Most helpful of all would be the introduction into these formal Type 3 processes of references to Type 2 opportunities and action plans. This relates very much to the last point about job moves, which will often be undertaken either as a result of a Type 3 analysis but more frequently offer Type 1 learning experiences because the reasons for them are purely managerial. Most opportunities for learning from the job will be identified between a manager and the subordinate. There is no reason at all, in fact every reason to the contrary, to separate these from Type 3 processes. In addition to the normal requests for formal development processes such as courses, job moves, appointments to committees or task forces, the kind of opportunities spelled out in the previous chapter can at least be referred to in this formal appraisal process.

There is no need for a long list of Type 2 opportunities or recent events; but the appraisal process should facilitate the continuing identification of opportunties and actions throughout the year. A review of managerial performance should therefore include a review of the extent to which Type 2 opportunities have been identified and plans undertaken to take advantage of them during the year. The reality of the managerial learning provided by Type 2 could be identified again, since the appraisal would concern itself not simply with achieved direct managerial results, but with the extent to which the manager involved has learned from success or failure. While this review should in the main be a day-by-day/week-by-week basis, it would be extremely valuable for it to be summarized, and perhaps planned, on a more forward-looking basis through the opportunity which a Type 3 appraisal process would provide.

SHIFTING THE BOUNDARIES IN APPRAISAL

One of the undoubted shifts over recent years has been away from a purely downwards judgemental review and feedback by the boss to a more participative process where boss and subordinate share the appraisal. This involves the subordinate in conducting some kind of self appraisal, sometimes by using the normal form and filling in the details for later comparison with the boss's views, sometimes the individual has a separate deliberately designed self-appraisal form.

While there can be problems about the degree of frankness and openness – particularly in organizations where these are not otherwise encouraged – self-appraisal, although it calls for additional skills from boss and subordinate, can be much more productive than a purely top-down appraisal.

A rather more recent development is a formal process by which the subordinate appraises the boss. This can work only in certain kinds of organization; some in which I have been employed would not have been able to cope. However, it can be very

productive in its discussion of how realistic a boss's perceptions of
his/her own performance are. Even more importantly, it can be
helpful in securing change by one or both parties.

There is the possibility of team appraisal. This was most
frequently encountered in the 1970s through organization development and process consultation, where teams reviewed their own
performance. It has been suggested by Margerison[4] that team
appraisal can be complementary to individual appraisal. I have not
encountered other references to this or seen examples of it in
practice, but in principle it seems attractive. It can raise issues which
individual appraisal does not and it has the advantage of recognizing
the reality that managerial work involves team as well as individual
achievement.

DIFFERENT PURPOSES, DIFFERENT ANSWERS

One of the difficulties is that different people have different
needs for different appraisal information at different places in the
organization. An answer which encourages effective individual
discussion between boss and subordinate is not equally useful to a
personnel man who wants to make a more effective resource and
succession plan. Given the inaccuracies inherent in the nature of
the discussion itself, i.e. the extent to which boss and subordinate
actually identify the appropriate issues, and the probable difficulties
of accurately recording what was actually said, it makes more sense
to give greater weight to objectives relating to the discussion itself
rather than the data produced. This leads towards a view of appraisal
as:

- a discussion about how and why the subordinate is presently
  performing in his job
- identifying how the subordinate might perform more effectively
- identifying ways in which he or she might set about performing
  more effectively
- occurring in a context which leaves the subordinate, boss and
  organization all satisfied that action is being taken to raise the
  level of individual performances.

MEASURING YOUR CURRENT POSITION

We have reviewed the major issues about appraisal. You might find it helpful to review your own position against each of the major headings identified. This is not an audit which can be satisfactorily achieved by giving yourself marks. The process might rather involve answering the following questions.

Exercise

1 On how many of these issues would I rate my current organization's position as satisfactory?
2 On how many would I find my organization's position unsatisfactory?
3 What major changes have occurred in our appraisal process over the last five years? What caused the changes?
4 How many explicit objectives do we have in our appraisal scheme? Do we have concealed or implicit objectives as well? Do they conflict with each other?
5 Who owns the appraisal scheme?
6 How far up the organization does formal appraisal go? Does the chief executive appraise his or her direct reports?
7 What is our position on the relationship of appraisal and judgement on salaries?
8 Is our appraisal process based on personality characteristics, performance/results, behaviours/skills? What is the reason for whatever basis we have chosen?
9 If you are setting up an appraisal scheme for the first time, on which of the potential objectives for such a scheme do you intend to focus?

REFERENCES

1 RANDELL G. *et al.*, *Staff appraisal*. IPM, 1984
2 LONG P. *Performance appraisal revisited*. IPM, 1986
3 ARGYRIS C. *Reasoning learning and action*. Jossey Bass, 1982
4 MARGERISON C. 'Team appraisal – leadership and organisation'. *Development Journal*. Vol 4, No 2, 1983

5 Potential, Promotion and Evaluation

POTENTIAL AND PROMOTION

These are linked but not synonymous issues. An individual needs to have potential for growth to work successfully when promoted to a higher level post. However, an employee can have potential for a range of different jobs, which do not involve promotion: a sales manager can move to a marketing manager's job which is evaluated as being at exactly the same level; for the move to be successful the manager involved needs to have the potential to acquire the skills necessary for effective performance in the new job.

There are, essentially, two factors involved:

- the capacity of the organization to identify the skills, knowledge and experience necessary to perform well in the jobs it currently has, and (a very important issue in some companies) jobs of a different kind it believes it may have in the future
- the organization's capacity to measure those aspects of individuals' current performance, and those capacities which they are thought to have, in a way which makes prediction about their future performances accurate

It would be an understatement to say that both these requirements present major difficulties. Job performance requirements ought to be identified through up-to-date reviews of the managerial content of existing jobs. Where such statements do not exist, then the organization is compounding its potential for error. It will obviously have had little basis for assessing the performance of current job holders and it will have nothing against which to assess the current abilities and future potential of individuals to do those jobs in the future.

There are major problems in making accurate judgements about the performance of individuals in relation to jobs different from those they currently occupy. There are problems in establishing a sound basis for judgement about current performance; the problems multiply when those judgements are used to predict performance in a different job. At least performance in a current job is being assessed by someone who has a responsibility for it and has grounds (however confused) for saying 'that is the performance I am looking for'. That same manager can also be reasonably expected to make a judgement about the potential of a subordinate to perform the manager's own job. But when a boss is asked to look further afield and to make predictions about performance further up the line, or in different functions, in different countries, in different divisions or in different sizes of organizations, judgement becomes extremely fallible.

For these reasons researchers and specialists often advise that the making of judgements about promotion and general potential should be separated from the normal appraisal process (Chapter 4). This is rarely done because most managers regard the connection between reviewing current performance and making predictions about the future as entirely logical (which it ought to be); moreover, many managers would be most unwilling to double the amount of time they give to considering such issues.

If the normal appraisal process includes judgements about potential, more sophisticated organizations will provide questions which are intended to focus on different aspects of a manager's performance. The more specific the focus of the normal appraisal process, the more necessary it is to provide some guidance to managers on the kind of things which might indicate potential. For instance, a manager may be very good at problem solving, but in the sense of solving tactical, operational – basically firefighting – problems. A section on promotion or potential might ask the reviewing manager to identify those aspects of problem solving which indicate the potential to operate in a more strategic, forward-looking way.

Formal schemes now often include other processes no longer within the control of the reviewing manager or the reviewer plus grandfather. We will now look at the most widely used of these.

- Some *psychological tests* purport to measure particularly significant characteristics. They may be helpful in measuring such dimensions as creativity, problem solving and adaptability. If these are deemed necessary characteristics for someone to be moved successfully into another job, and if the tests are valid, then the tests can make a contribution.

- *Panel or group interviews* are essentially similar to recruitment interviews, although they may deal with prospective potential rather than immediate appointments. Most research on these processes seems to indicate that they face most of the problems of normal selection interviewing, complicated by the difficulty of getting any group or panel actually to agree on criteria or on the process for the interview.

- *Informal identification processes* include asking line managers or staff advisers, particularly personnel people, to produce lists of people with potential. These lists can be generated by a review of existing appraisal information or by visits carried out by a personnel specialist charged with the responsibility of identifying 'high flyers'. In any combination, this kind of process leads to accusations of 'the old boy network', subjectivity and unfairness.

- *Management simulation processes* derive largely from officer selection analogies. This kind of process involves putting people through exercises which simulate the conditions of a job different from that currently held. The simulation may be very close – a carefully designed in-tray exercise – or it may be very distant, as with so-called leadership exercises. These usually involve some version of physical outdoor activities, in which the performance of individuals in either individual pursuits such as canoeing or abseiling or in a team activity can be closely monitored and assessed. When carefully designed against properly established criteria, simulation processes of this kind carry a degree of surface validity and provide at least some objective evidence. However, the greater their specificity and, therefore, their potential validity, the greater the expense involved in actually running them. The temptation is to use one of the existing general exercises or someone else's in-tray exercise – which takes us back to the recurring problem of validity.

- *Assessment centres* usually combine in-tray and other simulation processes with group discussion, group tasks and interviews. Again if these are designed against clear criteria, and particularly if they are established specifically for individual organizations, then they can provide useful objective evidence. The same qualification, namely that this is often an expensive process, applies. The assessment centre process can be used purely for judging potential, but it can also be used to establish development needs. It is therefore a particularly powerful tool, but like many tools it is dangerous or ineffective if improperly used. For that reason it is given a section on its own later in this chapter.

- *Intuitive methods* essentially comprise a senior manager, after collecting a variety of data about an individual, deciding that he or she 'has what it takes'. As in other areas of their work senior managers are sometimes right in their intuition. They tend to remember when they were right more often than when they were wrong. Whatever the merits of intuition, it is a process which leaves everyone, except the person with the intuition and the person about whom the intuition has been positive, unhappy and unconvinced.

- *Assignments and special responsibilities*. Situations in which individuals are put through particularly pressing or stressful new or additional responsibilities are a way of testing them for the future. These can include being sent to small units with no support or being sent to a different country or involved in projects outside the normal range of experience. These are variants on using normal appraisal, i.e. achieved performance, as the basis for making judgement. The difference is that assignments can be specially identified as having a particular relevance to a future job.

A particularly important example of this was seen when Reg Jones, the Chief Executive Officer at General Electric in the United States, set about planning his own succession. (This case is described in a little more detail on p. 92.) It essentially included giving stretching assignments and increased visibility to ten potential successors.

The evidence suggests that any organization which relies on only one of these possible methods is exposing itself to major risks in attempting to identify and plan for the movement of its individual managers, whether sideways or upwards. The methods an organization chooses to use will, of course, relate its level of sophistication about management development and other aspects of organizational culture. The confidence of managers in their own ability to make judgements about potential and promotability is rarely affected by data showing how fallible they are. This is because organizations do not normally carry out reviews of predictions that were made even two years earlier – let alone those which were made five years earlier – to establish at least some objective measure of managerial judgement. One piece of American research showed that in two successive years there was a 50 per cent turnround in a list of judgements made about individuals with outstanding growth potential. One reason for this is that judgements made about an individual very early in a managerial career are particularly likely to be unfounded, since virginal, high IQ people untouched by industrial experience may seem to have extraordinary potential. It was said of the Roman emperor Galba that 'no-one would have doubted his capacity as Emperor if he had never been placed in that position'.

The comments so far have all been made from the organizational perspective: how do organizations make the most successful judgements? But as Lee[1] shows, individuals themselves make major interventions in the process. They do so in part by their own decisions about whether they want to pursue jobs elsewhere in the organization, whether promotion or sideways moves. Some decide not to but do not necessarily indicate this to their organizations. Management mythology tends to concentrate much more on those who deliberately set out to be promoted. Such individuals then make judgements about how they are to secure promotion. They look for hints and information about the kind of activities and behaviour which are seen to lead to the promotion of people to the sort of jobs they fancy. Such individuals will tend to make themselves highly visible, will be greatly concerned about internal politics and will seek to form relationships of influence and attachment to others whom they think will be useful. Lee observed things in one particular organization which will be recognizable to many of us. Managers reviewing the question 'What do I have to do to get promotion?' saw three ways:

- a fairly large minority who believed they had to work hard at their narrow task
- a majority who believed they had to achieve at their narrow task, but also at other work-related activities
- a few who were concerned with other ways of creating the right impression in the right places

Lee's essential proposition is that 'textbook theory of promotion processes is based on abstract ideas about how formal systems should operate. As in most areas of management, this proves a poor guide to reality.'

In a much larger scale exercise conducted by London and Stumpf,[2] the dominant factor influencing choice was the decision maker's personal knowledge of the candidate or person recommending a candidate. As they also say, motivated, astute managers even without formal career planning programmes seek information about opportunities and make their interests known.

An additional dimension is given by the common requirement to identify 'high flyers'. This concept is based on the idea that a small number of people have significantly different (greater) potential from the generality of managers, that they can be identified early and that the benefits of doing so are that they can be put through processes of management development more quickly. As Hirsch has found from her research,[3] high flyer schemes seem to generate more problems than solutions. The basis for judgement of early potential is unsound. The allocation of particular distinction to a small group of people tends to create jealousies among others, not least because the criteria for such identification are either unknown or unrecognizable. All too often, being a high flyer and being put on a 'fast track' tends to mean that people are moved around quickly in a way which encourages superficial rather than substantially effective performance.

Then there is the question of the extent to which the organization can actually predict its future requirements. The process of quantitative planning, with replacement tables, succession plans and so on, is covered later in this chapter. Here we simply need to note the more qualitative difficulty of actually establishing what the needs are either for existing jobs as they may need to be done in five years' time or, even more problematically, for jobs that do not yet exist but may need to exist in the future. Again it is possible to generalize about the skills and competences that will be required and some ideas about the future are reviewed in the next chapter. Any attempt to get managers to envision the skills required for the future as a way of making more effective promotion decisions becomes very fraught. It is not an area in which most managers have much skill in assessment and only a few have the intellectual curiosity to be interested in the attempt.

You may like to test your own organization's procedures for identifying potential and promotion by an exercise.

Exercise

1 Which of the processes indicated above are used in my organization?
2 Which are the most important in practice?
3 Have we recently tested the accuracy of our predictions?
4 What could we do to improve our processes?

It must finally be noted that the potential and promotion of ethnic minorities and women is a special issue. We will look at this in greater detail in Chapter 10; but it is important to say here that even apparently objective processes for decision making can be invalidated in relation to these two groups by the often deeply held but inaccurate stereotypes of many managers.

ASSESSMENT CENTRES

Assessment centres now have a relatively lengthy history. In principle they go back to the officer selection processes adopted in the UK during the 1939–45 war. Until the 1980s assessment centres were mainly used for selection; the initial focus on selection for an immediate current job was sometimes broadened to include identification of potential for appointment to different and probably more senior jobs. The feedback on perceived performance which was inherent in the design of effective selection–directed assessment centres was gradually recognized as identifying individual development needs. Evidence about the effectiveness of such feedback for developmental purposes was either thin or negative. The idea of assessment centres focusing explicitly, and perhaps even primarily, on development was a logical extension.

The essence of the traditional selection–based assessment centre process was the use of a variety of simulations, exercises, tests, discussions and interviews. These were all directed towards the 'objective' evaluation of the performance of candidates against a desired list of skills or characteristics. The essential principles are those of the measurement of observed behaviour which is related to desired skills (preferably organization-specific), with judgements made by at least a proportion of independent assessors, and explicit feedback to participants.

The validity of this process for selection purposes, certainly when properly designed and implemented, is now well established (see Sackett and Ryan[4]). The value for the purposes of individual development, as compared with immediate selection or the identification of longer-term potential, has, however, been less well studied. It does seem clear that attempts to double up on objectives by adding development purposes to basic selection are unsuccessful. This should be no surprise to anyone who has been involved in any form of management training, where a similar confusion of objectives over development and performance assessment leads to failure in both objectives. So a simple association between selection and development is unlikely to be productive. From a development point of view, much the most successful experiences have been achieved where the centre process has been explicitly aimed at identifying individual development, normally – and sensibly – associated with individual career plans. However, if the career planning element becomes part of feedback into the organization's formal career planning process this can create another confusion of objectives. Individuals who may be prepared to participate honestly in a centre whose objective is their personal development may be less prepared to do so when they think that the results of their performance may provide material for later judgements against them.

Most work on the use of assessment centres for the identification of potential has been done with young and very junior managers, dating back particularly to the massive studies done in the American company, AT & T.[5] Accurate feedback early in their working lives enables individuals to make better judgements about the jobs they choose to do. While the success of such programmes in predicting potential seems to have been well demonstrated, their success in practice in helping people to make career choices does not seem to have been well researched, no doubt because such research would be extremely difficult to do.

Assessment centres which identify current performance levels, and consequently development needs, may be called career development workshops, or personal development workshops. Perhaps because this development is relatively new, research so far seems to indicate that such workshops, though highly valued by many participants, have not yet been proved to be effective. Again assuming that the programme has been well designed, the careful and valid identification of performance issues can be achieved. Beyond that, such workshops offer a substantial period of time to work on the development needs and allow those involved to produce their own plans for tackling these needs.

It is more difficult to show that they result in concrete action. Outside the positive and encouraging context of the workshop, back in managerial reality, the likelihood of plans being implemented will be significantly reduced. However, given the level of commitment actually generated by individuals on such programmes, it would seem unreasonable to presume that the failure rate would be as high as it is on normal management training programmes, where similar aspirations and plans might be developed. Because the workshop operates at a much more specific level, and probably at a greater level of detail than time usually allows on most courses, the success rate may actually be both quantitatively and qualitatively higher. How much higher it is, and at what cost in terms of resources, is something which needs to be assessed by the organization using the process. It would also need to look at why plans were not activated, if this turned out to be the case, and the extent to which this was due to the unrealistically high level of optimism generated on a workshop or to the organizational environment.

Boehm[6] gives an excellent review of some of these issues. The weakness of her article is that it does not bring out sufficiently the confusion and conflict over objectives which we indicated earlier (though she does point out that assessment centres designed for development probably need to be twice as long as those adopted for selection). An interesting particular case, with a detailed timetable, is given by Griffiths and Allen.[7] You may wish to clarify your understanding of assessment centres and their place in management development by the following exercise.

Exercise

1   Read the article by Boehm. Have you experienced the purposes she has described? Which might be applicable to your own organization? What weaknesses in your current processes might be remedied?
2   Read the article by Griffiths and Allen. If you were a manager in the organization described, what concerns would you have about your involvement in such a workshop? On the information given, would you see the workshop as being primarily about:
    • the improved capacity of the organization to meet its own objectives?
    • having improved information on which to base your own career plan?
    • clear identification of personal development needs, and plans to meet them?
3   Would you see any conflict between these three in your own feelings about the workshop?

It should finally be noted that existing descriptions of development centres rarely indicate that attention is given to the individual learning processes of participants. Most descriptions produce statements about the identification of performance needs and the production of personal development plans 'using a variety of development processes'. Specific, direct and individual attention is rarely paid to the learning process involved in carrying out any of the planned activities, and the likely differences in learning styles between individuals.

One exception is described by Povah.[8] (The general point about differing individual approaches to learning is covered in more detail in Chapter 11.)

CAREER PLANNING

This section concentrates on the organizational processes used to identify career stages and to plan managerial careers. Chapters 7 and 11 look in more detail at the ways in which organizational plans may be put into effect by individuals and ways in which individuals can take their own initiatives about their own careers.

An organization is usually concerned to arrange its managerial jobs in an ascending hierarchical ladder, with the planned progression of individuals up that ladder. Where an organization has carried out the kind of detailed job reviews indicated in this chapter and in Chapter 6, it is possible to establish a developmental hierarchy based on significant changes of content. That hierarchy may conveniently coincide with a hierarchy drawn up for the purposes of job evaluation, with an organization chart or with job values as reflected by salary. Not surprisingly, however, judgements made for these other purposes may not dovetail with career planning.

These significant stages, in a formal sense, will therefore vary with the nature and size of any particular organization. The five stages in Figure 5.1 will be found in many organizations, although the detailed descriptions employed are appropriate to commercial business.

Figure 5.1   Management Career Stages

Supervisory function – detailed control of 'direct' workers

Functional management – managing the work of a complete area such as sales or production, through supervisors or lower management

Cross-functional management – involving the management of a number of associated functions. Examples could be a production director responsible for manufacture, safety, quality

Profit centre management – involving full accountability for all the functions and both revenue and cost

Plural profit centre management – often at director level, involving a number of profit centres, e.g. separate companies, in a division or in a total group

---

In the Civil Service, local government or the National Health Service, the stages listed in Figure 5.1 will not be different. Readers from such organizations should tackle the following exercise:

Exercise

What are the major stages of careers in my organization, defined by significant changes in accountability and content of managerial jobs? Are they more, less, or much the same as the levels indicated in Figure 5.1?

Formal management development can then be designed to meet the changing needs of these different career stages, and can also be designed to incorporate the wishes of individual managers within the organization. When organizations talk about career planning, they are usually talking about taking people through different kinds of formal process which contribute to the development of individual careers, but are not necessarily linked to a formal career structure. From a practical point of view it is probably the case that effort is more sensibly directed at the particularities of jobs rather than grand statements about developing people for level 3 in a career plan. The more significant point is almost certainly the one we hinted at earlier: the organization's career planning process ought to be regarded as a complete system to do with managerial careers rather than just those aspects of it which are clearly addressed by development processes. An effective career plan will probably include issues outside the job responsibility of a management development adviser, but certainly the responsibility of a personnel director, and even more appropriately, the chief executive. The plan will include:

- *clear job descriptions*, which in addition to their basic managerial merits also provide clarity for identifying potential career moves
- *a reward system*, which provides both recognizably different financial and psychological satisfactions between levels
- *job selection processes* which provide equality of treatment between insiders and outsiders
- *blockage removal processes* which enable organizations to remove dead wood or live wood which is blocking the growth of even livelier wood

We must now return to the question of the individual's own

expectations. My research has shown how great the distance can be between what the organization was attempting in planning careers and what individuals have experienced. Individuals' views about their desired careers may be quite different from the organization's. Whatever the organization deems desirable in terms of total career plans, it should incorporate processes for finding out individuals' own views. I remember a case in an organization where I worked, in which our plans placed considerable emphasis on a move to be made by a functional manager into a profit centre management job (level 2 to level 4 on Figure 5.1). But the individual involved told me that not only did he not want to make the move, but that he had been quite unable to communicate this to his own boss, who kept insisting that it was 'the right move for you'.

The link between career planning and the previous sections on potential, promotion and assessment centres will no doubt be clear. If the processes you employ to determine achieved performance are not accurate, if your processes for reviewing potential are ineffective, and if as a consequence your ability to help individuals improve their performance is flawed, then career planning collapses from the weight it places on these crumbling foundations. Even where these organizational aspects are well designed, appropriate and successfully geared to identifying performance, the individual and his or her personal career ambitions, and particularly issues of personal growth and development, will still affect the implementation of any career plan. All too often career planning would work very well if only people were not involved. Chapter 7 takes a number of these issues further.

There is then the question of the 'plateaued' manager. The career plan must look at the issue of whether, at any particular level, there are managers who are either ineffective or who are effective but holding back managers with higher potential. While hard decisions may be necessary, sensible career planning will take account of the fact that most organizations need managers who have settled at a particular point. They may be referred to as 'solid citizens' or a 'safe pair of hands', but the probability is that they provide the stability, experience and commitment to a job which ensures that the organization survives. The needs of such managers, and the organization's need for them, must be incorporated in the career plan. An article by Davies and Deighan[9] provides useful guidance on this subject.

Here is an exercise through which you can test your own current situation and views:

Exercise

How far do we have a fully integrated system for career planning?
Does the integration include consideration of the non-management
development aspects mentioned above?

SUCCESSION PLANNING – OR IS IT
RESOURCE PLANNING?

There are organizations in which no one thinks about who will fill
managerial vacancies before they occur – but very few. There are
many more in which managers say 'of course we give some thought
to it, but I could not say we have a plan as such'. If you pursue the
'as such' you find that what they mean is that from time to time
they have conversations about what might happen if X left job Y,
or else someone confesses that he is going for a job interview with
another employer and managers then think about what they will
do if they have to replace him. Sometimes there is a level of concern
about the performance of an existing job holder and there is again
discussion about who might take over if that particular manager is
moved out.

Because such discussions are obviously loose, rarely address
the issues on a longer time-scale and are subject to the accident of
who is known by whom, they cannot properly be called succession planning. Yet maybe we have been too dismissive of this
idea in the past. It is certainly an inadequate process in most
organizations. The idea that an organization will have to plan
the replacement of capital equipment well ahead, with careful
identification of performance requirements, but that such a process
is either unnecessary or impossible for managerial resources, should
not be readily accepted. But what we should do is build on what
managers will be interested in doing naturally, rather than ignoring
it. If managers can be persuaded to take an interest in issues of
succession through real problems as they occur, we should use that
as the basis for an argument in favour of planning to fill managerial
positions.

My study of successful management development schemes
shows that in most, although not all cases, the successful introduction of planning has derived from what I call 'felt hurt'. (Indeed,

this is also true for formal management development in total.) Attempts to introduce succession planning 'because company X does it', or 'because companies of our size normally do this sort of thing' or 'because I have done a study of management development systems in other companies, and this is an area of weakness for us' are less likely to be effective. If we start from where managers are we are more likely to engage their interest and attention even in formal processes than if we start from our management development or personnel professionalism which indicates what a company 'ought' to do.

The basic concepts of Succession Planning are simple, which is no doubt why they have been followed by a good many organizations. There are various ways of setting out what is

Figure 5.2 Company *X* – Succession Plan

Job/Current holder	Succession within 2 yrs	Sucession 2–5 yrs	Comments	Suggested action
Divisional chairman (David X)				
Divisional chairman (Derek Y)				
Finance director (Sydney G)				
Production director (John S)				
Sales director (Brian B)				
Personnel director (Paul M)				

involved and securing the information necessary. Figure 5.2 is a relatively simple one which I developed for one organization.

Some organizations produce much more complex statements, with colour coding indicating functional or product experience, age, and items like job ranking or evaluation score.

To support this kind of plan (which without the action plan column completed is a statement of intention rather than a plan) a complementary document may be produced which takes people rather than jobs as its prime focus. This will, in fact, deal with the question of a career plan for individuals of the kind indicated in the previous section. An illustration, again deliberately in a relatively simple form, is given in Figure 5.3.

Figure 5.3   Company *X* – People Plan

	Career progression within 2 yrs	Career progression 2–5 yrs	Comments	Suggested action
David X				
Derek Y				
Sydney G				
John S				
Brian B				
Paul M				

WHICH JOBS, WHICH PEOPLE?

An organization may have to decide which jobs to consider and which people to consider for which jobs. An issue which tends to cause considerable debate is whether all the jobs at a particular level are considered in the succession planning process: they normally are. The associated question is whether all the job holders are considered as part of the plan; in other words whether the list of people for career progression is exactly the same as the list of job holders. Here there are two problems. The first is that some job holders may be considered to be 'plateaued' or even, indeed, beyond their peak and therefore not worthy of consideration in a succession planning routine. The second problem is that there will be people with potential at levels beneath those covered by the jobs under consideration. This may in practice be covered by a separate list – known colloquially as the 'high flyer' list, whatever formal title such as 'longer-term potential' it is given within the organization.

The list of jobs to be considered in some organizations will be self evident; some are small enough for the whole managerial population to be reviewed. In large multinationals with thousands of managers this is clearly impossible. Because of their huge size Unilever and BP make judgements about succession and career planning through committees which consider people at different levels. Perhaps the most characteristic phenomenon is that of an organization which reviews its top layer of jobs, which often seems to fall between 30 and 70. It will have a similar but not identical list of people and it is by making decisions about these two groups that the tables illustrated in Figures 5.2 and 5.3 are filled in.

The process by which the plan is produced and discussed varies between organizations, but some fairly common elements are:

- Collection of information from appraisals of the individuals concerned (where they exist)
- summarizing of that information, often by the personnel function
- alternatively the line manager is presented with a chart empty of everything except the name of the job and job holder, and is then asked to insert his comments on the blank, or to talk through his comments with a personnel adviser
- the information collected is then put together in a file or binder and is presented to a decision-making group or to the chief executive alone
- the group or chief executive reviews the comments made and makes a final decision about the comments recorded on the succession plan
- the process by which the succession plan is eventually reviewed and adopted often includes either a special meeting of the board or management committee, or involves a special management development committee created for the purpose. In either case the significance of the process and the decision-making intensity are quite often registered by holding such a meeting off site, normally in a pleasant residential setting

Sadly, for some organizations this is a purely paper exercise. In spite of all the trouble that the organization seems to have gone to, the actual process of deciding succession frequently takes place as if the succession plan had never been produced. I suspect that the well intentioned process of taking people away from their normal workplace actually contributes to this, because it makes the whole thing so different from normal managerial decision making. Of course the intention is to enable people to concentrate fully on this very important issue, rather than being distracted by phone calls or 'the likelihood of us being forced to attend to normal business issues'.

Another reason for the relative ineffectiveness of many succession plans is that they are initially designed and drafted by personnel people. The question of ownership mentioned in Chapter 2 applies strongly here. Making succession plans is too often seen as a purely personnel activity, not one owned by line management.

Paradoxically the greater the level of influence and sophistication of personnel, the more likely it is that they will produce and carry out, for at least a period of time, a succession planning process which line managers regard as too complicated.

Of course some organizations are successful, but consideration of causes of failure will perhaps help others avoid error. My own experience is that the succession planning process is in fact rather too easily adopted by some line mangers. It is a great relief to be able to make hypothetical decisions, rather than to engage with the sordid reality of decisions which have immediate consequences.

One successful case is the experience of General Electric in the United States. Some years ago its then Chief Executive, Reg Jones, identified as one of his prime concerns that there should be an internal candidate identified and developed for his job before he retired. He himself described the process he went through. This first of all involved drawing up a list of ten people with high potential. This was narrowed down to three before his eventual successor, Arthur Walsh, was chosen and put in place. One interesting point here is the number of potential people who were considered. (Another is that they were tested by stretching assignments.)

It is sensible here to repeat a familiar message: decisions will only be as good as the information on which they are based. Alternative sources of information are listed in the section on potential. My own experience has been that the collection of information from a variety of sources has helped make decisions more realistic, but that the sheer volume of papers can be unmanageable. As an adviser I therefore developed a process of producing shorter pen pictures of the individuals involved in a succession plan. These summarized all the information available, from appraisal, psychological assessment, personal development discussions, even to oral comments where these had been given by the individual's manager on some serious occasion (as compared with off-the-cuff comments made on a site visit).

A RESOURCE PLAN

In most organizations the real issue is not succession, or certainly not solely that. The real management development concern ought to be the performance of managers in their current jobs. It is more sensible to think in terms of a resource plan than a succession plan.

The resource plan embraces a review of all current jobs and job holders and causes responsible managers to review whether current performance is satisfactory with a wide-angle lens rather than the narrow focus on a particular individual which is the purpose of individual appraisal. The review is then directed neither at hypothetical succession needs – 'if *X* falls under a bus' – nor even at explicit age-based needs, but is directed at issues of immediate direct concern to senior managers. Making a resource plan is certainly a less comfortable process, because it is not about hypothetical decisions which may never need to be acted on. It requires managers to deliver a verdict on the success or otherwise of managers in their current jobs. The great virtue of the process is precisely that it deals with reality. Although it is more uncomfortable it is accepted by managers as more meaningful, providing there is an existing level of interest and concern about managers' current performance.

As with appraisal, we here pass over a vast volume of detail about alternative versions of succession plans or resource plans; see Further Reading for more. The main issue here is clarification of purpose; it is not really a question of whether we can design clever forms, but whether we can design and implement a process which provokes not only interest but effective action from line managers.

The following exercise may usefully test out your ideas on these issues.

Exercise

1 What do we have at the moment in terms of planning our future management succession?
2 If we have had formal plans, have we checked to see whether they are used when vacancies arise?
3 Do we have a clear plan at least for those jobs which will arise through retirement?
4 Is the concept of a succession plan attractive to my managers, or would they be more likely to respond to the challenge of a resource plan?

RECRUITMENT AND SELECTION

When I went to talk to a general manager my company had recruited from outside about the development of his people, his response was brusque. 'I won't mention sows; but I will say that I can't make good products out of poor materials.' The section on career planning has indicated the significance of recruitment and selection policies: there is very little point in planning internal careers if that planning is thwarted by quite different recruitment and selection policies. In the context of this book, these are the crucial points about recruitment and selection. We do now recognize in management development that training and development can be the wrong answer to some managerial problems, which have nothing to do with the level of skill and a great deal to do with other sources of managerial failure. Similarly, formal management development processes may help to remedy weaknesses in managers once selected, but they cannot deal with a totally inappropriate selection.

EVALUATING THE SYSTEM

Remarkably little work has been done on assessing whether the system works; even articles which set out to describe the system often turn out to be describing the effect of courses.

The fundamental questions to ask about the effectiveness of management development schemes are:

- Does the scheme achieve what it sets out to achieve? (Answering this question, particularly in relation to courses, has often been described as 'validation'.)
- Has the process produced results in terms of the demonstrated effectiveness of managers?

Our research on the development of directors took us into some very large organizations which had been carrying out management development for many years. At that time none of them had made a formal analysis of the effectiveness of their scheme, either overall or in terms of whether it provided for succession to the main board. One of the major reasons for this is contained in the first of the two questions above. Few of them had established any measurable objective for their schemes, or specified the particular achievements they desired from individual management development processes. Without such objectives it is very difficult to evaluate management development systems.

It is easier to assess particular parts of the system. Some

organizations do this for courses, or the achievements of the formal appraisal scheme. Naturally enough, if the inputs, i.e. the elements of the system, have not been reviewed, then any claims that may be made about the system producing more effective managers (the second issue mentioned above) will be extremely suspect. Managers' effectiveness might have nothing at all to do with formal systems of management development; and indeed that was the burden of the evidence presented to us by a number of directors in our research.

The only other research in the UK was conducted by Easterby-Smith and his colleagues in the late 1970s.[10] Although the particular approach they described was lengthy and resource consuming, it is perhaps surprising that the major principles used in their audit approach seem not to have been subsequently taken up by organizations. Their approach involved managers in the organizations reviewed in assessing the extent to which management development systems were actually influencing development. A cynic might take the view that since their research showed, as did mine later, that systems were much less effective than the personnel owners believed, there is every reason for personnel people not to sponsor evaluation processes.

The questions used in my own study of systems were (excluding specifics about directors):

Exercise

1 Do you have a policy or statement about developing managers?
2 Have these policies or systems changed significantly over the last fifteen years? If so, how?
3 What stimulated any changes?
4 Have there been partial or smaller-scale initiatives within the total system which have been important (e.g. a particular process or activity)?
5 Is there anything else about the history of management development in your organization which will help us understand the comments we will receive?
6 How significant have formal processes been in developing managers as compared with informal processes?
7 Do you have any prospective changes to your management development processes in mind?
8 How do you evaluate your investment in management development?

You may work for an organization which has already evaluated its management development system. If this has not in fact been done, then you could benefit from providing your own individual answers to the above questions.

You might then consider whether to set up a more substantial process of assessing your scheme either by a small-scale exercise conducted by yourself with a selected number of managers, or by conducting a more rigorous review probably involving an outside consultant, in order to be fully objective. As part of the process of deciding whether you want to undertake a more sophisticated review you should look at the book by Easterby-Smith already referred to, and also at his later publication.[11]

The main focus of this section so far has been on meeting the first purpose of evaluation: does the system actually operate in the way intended? The second issue is clearly whether it secures desirable results. There are some problems about what is meant by results. Here is a list of a number of things which might be intended, and actually produced:

- improved competence in the existing job
- competence developed in advance of a future job
- more effective career decisions
- turnover of managers at the level desired by the organization (which might be nil or 50 per cent)
- enhanced commitment to the purposes of the organization
- reduction of frustration within individual jobs
- increased satisfaction within individual jobs.

As far as most line managers are concerned, the real question is whether formal management development processes affect desired organizational performance; this is referred to in commercial organizations as 'the bottom line'. The evidence on this is again extremely scanty. Although *In search of excellence*,[12] for instance, says that excellent companies give more attention to management training and development, they do not show any direct correlation between excellence and management development. This is also true of the fifteen excellent companies identified by Kotter,[13] who gives rather more detail on the management development processes the companies actually use; again his research seems to show a coincidence rather than a correlation between good management development practices and excellent company performance.

We finally turn to national reports on management development. These have usually become attached to the names of the prime authors, starting with Mant[14] on the experienced manager through to the reports of Professor Charles Handy and Professor John Constable in 1987.[15] Mant's report really describes the desirability and relative effectiveness of different approaches to management development. Handy and Constable are in a different but now long-standing tradition of criticizing the amount of management development undertaken; Handy is also concerned with content. Although valuable in many respects, the reports do not contribute substantially to the issue of evaluation.

A report by PA[16] in 1986 which looked at formal schemes in eight countries again confirmed the major validation problem. Only 46 per cent of respondents from 200 organizations with formal schemes, thought them totally or largely successful. As a matter of national comparison it is perhaps interesting that 68 per cent of the respondents in the UK claim to have a formal scheme, whereas the figures are only 26 per cent in France and 34 per cent in West Germany. Given the relative success of the economies of these two countries, it might again be thought that evidence of the ultimate effectiveness of management development schemes is somewhat lacking. This would, however, be too harsh a conclusion to draw from a single survey.

Issues on the evaluation of courses are covered in Chapter 8.

Exercise

1 What are the greatest strengths, and the greatest weaknesses, of my organization's processes for establishing potential?
2 What are the greatest strengths, and the greatest weaknesses in our promotion processes?
3 Do we do succession planning or resource planning? Is what we are doing satisfying the real needs of our organization?
4 Which of the possible steps identified for evaluating our management development system would it be most sensible for me to take?

REFERENCES

1 LEE R. 'The theory and practice of promotion processes'. *Leadership and Organisation Development Journal*. Vol 6, No 2 and Vol 6, No 4, 1985

2   LONDON M. and STUMPF S. 'How managers make promotion decisions'. *Journal of Management Development*. Vol 3, No 1, 1984

3   HIRSH W. *'Career management in the organisation'*. IMS Report No 96, 1984

4   SACKETT P. R. and RYAN A. M. 'A review of recent assessment centre research'. *Journal of Management Development*. Vol 4, No 4, 1985

5   *ibid*

6   BOEHM V. R. 'Using assessment centres for management development'. *Journal of Management Development*. Vol 4, No 4, 1985

7   GRIFFITHS P. and ALLEN B. 'Assessment centres: breaking with tradition'. *Journal of Management Development*. Vol 6, No 1, 1987

8   POVAH N. 'Using assessment centres as a means for self development'. *Industrial and Commercial Training*. March/April 1986

9   DAVIES J. and DEIGHAN Y. 'The managerial menopause'. *Personnel Management*. March 1986

10 EASTERBY-SMITH M., BRANDEN E. and ASHTON D. *Auditing management development*. Gower, 1980

11 EASTERBY-SMITH M. *Evaluation of management education training and development*. Gower, 1986

12 PETERS T. and WATERMAN R. *In search of excellence*. Harper and Row, 1982

13 KOTTER J. P. *The leadership factor*. Free Press, 1988

14 MANT A. *The experienced manager – a major resource*. BIM, 1969

15 HANDY C. *The making of managers*. NEDO, 1987; and CONSTABLE J. *The making of British managers*. BIM/NEDO, 1987

16 PA CONSULTANTS, *Management development*. PA, 1986

6 Establishing Development Needs

The previous chapters have looked at the range of processes used within the formal system for assessing the current performance and future potential of managers. Brief reference has been made to the issue of the definition of the required skills and competences and ways in which these formal review processes can sharpen the assessment of current skill levels.

This chapter starts by building on those formal review processes such as appraisal, potential review and assessment centres, which focus primarily on individual performance. Then we move to processes which start from a more general and external view of what development needs might be, now or in the future. This leads to some comments about what might be called the macro-learning process – the learning organization.

INFORMAL BUT IMMEDIATE PROCESSES

The most extreme form of unguided identification of needs occurs when a manager identifies a performance weakness in a subordinate and immediately suggests that action should be taken on it. This immediacy of diagnosis and action is certainly realistic in terms of normal managerial processes, but is prone to the same weaknesses, in both diagnosis and solution, as many other normal managerial activities. The manager may assess as a weakness something that is not a weakness or attribute the weakness to an irrelevant cause. This kind of instant diagnosis rarely engages the subordinate in a shared discussion of either the problem or solution, which may itself bring additional problems later in persuading the subordinate to believe the statement of need or accept the proposed solution.

Examples of such statements range from 'I think we should

send you on an interpersonal skills course; that last discussion with Jack showed that you use too much aggression and create opposition to your ideas' to 'I am sending you out with Jean to pick up everything she knows about this new product that you are taking over'. It will be noted that in both these examples the statement of the solution precedes the statement of the problem. This is characteristic of managers who operate in this way: they are dealing with a managerial problem not something they define as a training or learning need.

Many Type 1 learning processes derive from these kind of statements. They are an inevitable and proper way of identifying needs, though obviously they are not formal processes of identification which would be regarded as 'good' in a formal management development process. We have created problems for ourselves in management development by attempting to replace these admittedly rough and unsatisfactory processes rather than building on them. The weaknesses of diagnosis and commitment have to be weighed against the advantages of immediacy and reality.

BLANK PAGE PROCESSES

In Chapter 4 we reviewed the possible content of appraisal forms, particularly how much guidance should be offered on the specifics of performance and skill. Sometimes managers claim that they would prefer a simple blank page approach, and indeed some schemes provide very little guidance on the grounds that it is better to make managers think about the words they have to write than it is to provide organized but mechanical checklists either of headings or of explicit skills.

I once worked with a newly appointed chief executive who, while prepared to appraise at least some of his subordinates, disliked the existing appraisal form. He thought that the headings were in some cases inappropriate for the level he was to review and in others a mental straitjacket. I redesigned the form for him so that it simply asked him to review:

- current performance against objectives
- reasons for current performance
- steps necessary to improve performance
- potential for promotion
- reasons for prediction
- development needs – current and future

His first reaction was that he had asked for a blank page, but that he supposed that I was right to divide it up with the headings I had suggested. He used the form with two of his subordinates and came back to me. He had discovered that although he could complete the form and have what he regarded as a good discussion, it was taking him a long time to think his way into the issues. So he decided that he did want something which gave him some clues about the particular aspects he should be thinking about.

SKILLS- OR BEHAVIOUR-BASED INDIVIDUAL APPRAISAL

The appraisal form, or the document used in an assessment centre, can contain lists of desired qualities, skills, behaviours, competences. The effective analysis of needs depends on such lists being appropriate to the particular organization rather than generalized. The ways in which such lists can be produced are covered in a later section. For the moment we need only look at the advantages of such lists. The lists may be indicative: 'Think about the following dimensions in completing your appraisal', or prescriptive: 'Give your rating on each of the following required management skills'.

Chapter 4 discussed the problems of the personal qualities approach in appraisal. It is precisely in the area of development needs that such assessments collapse. The problems of providing appropriate learning experiences in order to develop characteristics such as 'dependability', 'initiative', 'energy', 'judgement' are massive. Most appraisal schemes therefore now try to focus on performance, behaviour and skills.

THE USE OF OBJECTIVES, KEY RESULT AREAS, PRIORITIES

A preliminary step favoured by many organizations, both for the conduct of appraisal and for identifying needs, is to establish the achieved level of performance against major output requirements. The useful residue of the management-by-objectives movement of the 1960s and 1970s, this essentially provides a rational basis on which to make a judgement about development needs. However, it provides only the basis; it does not indicate detailed requirements. Knowing, for example, that a manager 'failed to achieve the agreed objective on quality' indicates an area for discussion rather than a development need. Is the cause of failure the fact that the manager did not know enough about quality as a subject, or enough about the technical processes necessary to ensure it, or that his relationships with other departments were bad, or that the materials coming in to the plant were substandard, or that he was under pressure from the sales department to release defective goods? The great virtue of starting from such issues is that they focus on real managerial concerns, which both parties to the discussion will usually agree are real. They are much less likely to dismiss the subsequent discussion, and any development needs which may be identified, as 'an unreal exercise about learning needs'.

INDIVIDUAL DEVELOPMENT PLANS

So far all the processes illustrated have essentially been part of the direct relationship between the manager and subordinates, with managerial judgements made about development needs. An alternative is to bring in a third party. This involves an internal or external adviser in a preliminary discussion with an individual manager. The results of that discussion are then taken back into the line system; it is crucial that the role of the third party is seen as facilitating the eventual discussion and not replacing it. A skilled facilitator will draw out more from the manager involved, and probably also be aware of a greater variety of potential development solutions, than most line managers. This is a relatively expensive process and has therefore been used either for senior management positions, as described by Mumford[1] and Rose[2] or to meet a substantial change in business purpose, as described by Cunningham and Leon.[3]

GENERALIZED PROCESSES OF IDENTIFYING NEEDS

So far the emphasis has been on processes which are specific to the individual and to the organization. Of course, the indicative or prescriptive lists of skills or behaviours required are general to the extent that they are used with all managers. The methods by which such lists are produced vary between organizations. Some will have carried out a detailed analysis of required skills. A list is produced, perhaps by the use of relatively unstructured open-ended interviewing techniques, by more sophisticated repertory grid techniques, by managerial skill checklists, by discussions among groups of managers, or by some combination of these. It may be specific to a particular unit or division or to the whole organization. Some good ideas on these approaches, and specifics on possible resulting content, are given by Andrew Stewart.[4]

An alternative approach is to use an already existing list. One easily available example is given in the book on self-development by Pedler and his colleagues.[5]

The competency approach has emerged in recent years. The book by Boyatzis[6] gives the full results of his research, with information from 2,000 practising managers in 41 different types of jobs in a dozen different organizations. The end result was a set of 18 competency descriptors, separated into four clusters. The clusters were:

- goal and action management
- directing subordinates
- human resource management
- leadership

I have used the full set of descriptors in working with managers to assess their required level of performance and their current level of ability. Some discussions arise about some of the language used in the descriptors, but in general I have found it a powerful tool. In fact I prefer the Boyatzis list to the one produced by the Training Agency and the Council for Management Education and Development in 1988. My basic reason is that I believe that the Boyatzis descriptors are more valid because they are research-based.

The concept of competencies is itself one which is not accepted as valuable by all management development practitioners. Some would prefer to focus on explicit skills and behaviours, rather than attempting to imply a definition which seems to include not only skill but aspects of knowledge, accompanied by psychological aspects of 'willingness'. I share with Burgoyne[7] major reservations about the practicability and desirability of using the competency approach on a national basis. It is fair to say that a competency approach used with discretion by an organization, i.e. adjusted and interpreted to suit that organization's actual situation could be more helpful than simply doing nothing or starting from scratch.

See now Chapter 13 for further discussion of this issue.

GENERALIZED SKILLS OR COMPETENCIES?

The problem essentially is that we want a convenient and economic answer and that at the same time we would like it to be an accurate reflection of reality in our particular organization. Yet as Hirsh found in her major study,[8] there is not only widespread disagreement between organizations, on what the crucial skills are, but significant disagreement on what the same word means. Good decision making in one company means taking innovative decisions whereas in another it means working from hard data and minimizing risk.

WHAT MANAGERS REALLY DO

We constantly return to the fact that managerial life and required managerial performance differ from one organization to another; any generalized list is likely to be at least partially inapplicable. Lists of skills and competencies also suffer from the major disadvantage that they are too neat and discrete. Although it is convenient to separate things out for analysis, and to some extent also appropriate to work on individual issues such as the skills of interviewing or analytical approaches to decision making, managerial life is not separated into neat boxes.

We can only be surprised and saddened by the apparent continuing failure of many authors, or business schools and management training centres, to define and implement their offerings in terms of what managers actually do. The fundamental work of Rosemary Stewart,[9] Henry Mintzberg[10] and John Kotter[11] has not, it seems, been widely adopted by management developers, management educators or trainers. All three of these authors are descriptive rather than prescriptive. Their views are radically different from those of the classical theorists like Fayol and his successors through to Urwick, Brech and many subsequent imitators. These writers were essentially prescriptive: they said that managers should behave in particular ways in order to be effective. They further presumed that effective managerial processes were essentially the same for all managers in all kinds of organizations.

The contribution of Stewart, Mintzberg and Kotter is in many ways fundamental. It is central to our problem of defining what it is that we want managers to be able to do. It must also be remembered that their approach was based on reviewing the reality of how managers performed using interviewing, diary-keeping and observation techniques, rather than relying on detailed questionnaires or hypothetical constructs about how managers might behave if they were not answering a questionnaire. Their conclusions have a great deal in common, although Stewart collected data for hundreds of managers and Mintzberg and Kotter observed and interviewed only small numbers. Management development advisers should preferably read these three books (or at least the articles written by Mintzberg[12] and Kotter).[13] A convenient summary is provided in Mumford.[14]

In terms of the assessment of needs, and certainly of working on real issues subsequently, the Stewart, Mintzberg and Kotter material is very powerful and useful. The answers they give may sometimes lack clarity, but this is because they are describing the reality in which managers work. Their material is therefore particularly valuable where you may be working with an individual manager on analysing his own job. I have also found it of particular value on some management courses,[15] where the process of helping individuals to establish their own development needs is a significant requirement (see Chapter 11 for further discussion of this).

LEADERSHIP OR MANAGEMENT?

The development of the concept of leadership has been an obvious trend in the management development world, with some particularly startling statements about it being made in the 1980s. The idea has moved on from the days of simple comparisons with military forms of leadership in the 1950s, through the early days of appraisal schemes which asked people to assess others on undefined concepts of leadership. We now have much more sophisticated, and indeed demanding statements, exemplified by, for example, Bennis[16] and Kotter.[17] The concept of some special form of direction provided by leadership is undoubtedly attractive to many managers. Part of the attraction lies in being someone who goes to Ascot as compared with ordinary races: it is an indication of higher class status. The word implies other concepts such as 'vision', 'charisma' and most recently, 'transformational leadership'. Bennis talks about the transformational leader as one who creates and articulates a vision, shaping and elevating the motives and goals of his followers.

If you take the view that leadership is separate and distinct

from management, then it could represent a different level or type
of development need. The books referred to will help the reader
decide whether that is indeed an appropriate road. My own view
is that it is not. To attribute to the manager only the most routine,
basic and least exciting parts of the direction of his unit or
organization, while attributing all the stimulating, creative and
direction-changing processes to the leader is to demean the managerial process itself.

CHANGING REQUIREMENTS

Emphasis has so far been placed on identifying real needs in existing
job performance. However, this form of analysis needs to be
supplemented by considering three ways in which individual
development needs have to respond to more than current circumstances. The first of these is changes in skill requirements in the
current job. Perhaps the most dramatic examples of this have
occurred in the 1980s with the privatization of public sector
organizations. The changed requirements in, for example, British
Airways and British Telecom are referred to later in this chapter.
In other areas of our life, too, there have been major shifts of
emphasis even if not of ownership, as in the National Health
Service and large areas of local government. Those skills which
managers required under the previous arrangements may no longer
be as important and they may need to acquire other skills such as
financial discipline and the ability to relate to customers.

The discussion of promotion in the previous chapter highlighted another important issue of succession. It is sometimes
possible to identify a very specific job or type of job for which a
manager is destined, and then to assess his or her current levels of
skill and experience against the requirements of the upcoming job.
It may be that the requirement is to extend or develop further
existing skills and knowledge; but promotion often brings with it
new and different responsibilities and skill requirements.

Substantial as the problems of predicting potential and establishing development needs against existing jobs are, the uncertainties
involved in trying to develop skills for unknown future jobs are
even more frightening. There has been no shortage over the last
twenty years of predictions about changes in management skill
requirements; but these have usually been offered at a general
level. Inevitably, they also tend by definition to reflect informed
guesswork rather than analysis of the new jobs since these do not

yet exist. The clearest examples of the creation of new jobs in the last ten or twenty years are of course in the technological field. We are now witnessing the evolution of managerial jobs in information technology, accompanied by the need for managers to understand the technology involved and its application even though they are not directly managing it.

Since it is difficult to be precise about what is needed in these areas, the pressing issue from a management development point of view becomes that of providing processes which as far as possible give analogous experiences. An example of this would be enabling managers to cope with future change by helping them to learn more effectively from the changes to which they are currently exposed. This issue is developed further in Chapter 7.

The reader may care to test current practices and possibilities against the individual-centred methods listed above.

Exercise

1   Which methods do we currently use?
2   Which seem to give greatest return in terms of willing participation of our managers?
3   Which serve the overall purposes of our formal management development scheme most effectively?
4   What changes, if any, could we consider within a particular method, or which additional methods might we consider using?

BUSINESS-CENTRED NEEDS IDENTIFICATION

Some of the most powerful definitions of need have arisen in organizations using a different process. The parallel is with needs arising from individual objectives and priorities, as illustrated earlier. Needs can be identified through, and generated by, changes in organizational objectives and priorities. One kind of example has already been given, the transformations in managerial require-ments in organizations moving from the public to the private sector, or substantially influenced by some organizational imperative. It may be that a substantial transformation in the perceived purpose of the business, or of its managerial requirements to meet those purposes, requires the development of a new range of skills. An interesting example is given by Bruce.[18] He describes part of the shift of attitude required in British Airways following the identification that customer service, not price, would give them a competitive edge.

The process used by myself and Peter Honey at Ford (see Chapter 7) involved managers more directly in establishing needs on a more personal basis, rather than simply participating (desirable though this is) in the identification of overall needs. As part of their shift towards a more participative style, and the use of a form of matrix management, we designed a development programme which required managers to analyse the need for changed behaviour.

In more steady-state organizations, identification of needs may still derive from the push of general business requirements as well as from individual-centred initial analysis. In its most characteristic form it nowadays derives from the organization's formal business plan. The people who write the formal business plan are required to consider management resource and skill implications, with consequent management development consequences. This may be expressed in terms like 'we need to enhance our marketing skills in order to generate new and more effective marketing plans', or 'our proposals for enhanced quality management mean that we will need to recruit a senior level manager, and train all our production managers to meet the new standards'.

In some organizations the requirement that management resourcing and development implications should be written into the plan itself does not exist. In those cases a concerned individual, probably a personnel director or a management development adviser, has to go through the plan and draw out the implications. In the previous chapter we looked at management resource planning in terms of identifying individuals for particular jobs; but it may be that the adviser will have to identify the skills needs arising from proposed changes in the business, rather than emphasizing the processes necessary for appointing managers to new or enhanced jobs.

The plan may stimulate a shift from a national and geographic organization to a product-based one, or a decision to devolve responsibility to identified profit centres because of projected growth in business. A few organizations even manage to plan their organizational changes sufficiently far ahead for the development of managers to occur before the change. Sadly, it is more likely that an organization will decide to devolve more responsibility and create more profit centres, and only begin to recognize needs when weaknesses are identified in the managers in post. This seems to have been the case in the National Health Service, where the imperative of organizational change preceded the development of managers capable of operating the new organization successfully.

In an action learning mode, it is possible to use the process of drawing up the business plan to create an awareness of, and indeed specifically identify, the skills and behaviour required to implement the plan. This process is described by Seekings and Wilson.[19]

NEEDS OR WANTS

One of the basic issues for individuals is whether what may be objectively recognized as needs actually exist as subjectively felt wants. On a macro-scale the same issue obtains for organizations. Objective, analytical, well based statements of what managers need in order to be effective can be treated with impatience or disrespect or simply not prioritized in terms of resources.

This is a frequent experience for management trainers and educators. Managers all too often arrive on courses with no analysis at all of their individual needs having been undertaken or, where an analysis of some kind has been done, without any commitment to it. If we add to this a disbelief in the efficacy of courses in general or in the ability of this particular course to meet the need, then the likelihood of success is predictably and actually low. The ideas usually described in management literature as 'expectancy theory' have been used by Charles Handy[20] to produce what he calls the 'motivation calculus':

- the strengths or salience of the need
- the expectancy that energy or effort will lead to a particular result
- the instrumentality of that result in reducing the need shown at the first line above

We should, however, emphasize that however sophisticated the process by which we try and establish needs by detailed job analysis, lists of competencies or skills, indulgence in the futurology of management expertise, little is likely to happen unless we seriously engage managers themselves in the process.

It is relevant that cold-blooded, logical analyses of the kind largely illustrated here bear little relationship to what managers actually do when they are managing. It is for this reason that the approach through performance – perhaps through the achievement of objectives – is likely to be more attractive and therefore more successful than an approach through skills. It is similarly the reason why, at the large-scale organizational level, the identification of particular problems and concerns, whether through a formal business plan or simply through the recognition of a need for a major change, is again likely to be more effective than some of the more coolly considered and specifically learning-centred approaches illustrated earlier.

This is why I tend to approach this whole process from the view that managers respond to what I call 'felt hurt'. If we deal with the things which worry them we stand the risk of being superficial, it is true; but we acquire the great benefit of dealing with things which are of significant concern to them. The danger of emphasizing cool, rational analysis is that it will produce needs which objectively are excellently defined, but which unfortunately fail to attract the interest of those we need to respond.

USING LEARNING OPPORTUNITIES TO DEFINE NEEDS

The model of management development offered in this book includes those informal and accidental experiences described as Type 1. The emphasis so far in this chapter on wholly formal processes of identifying needs should be supplemented by an understanding of how these Type 1 experiences themselves can create a better recognition of needs, which can in turn lead to Type 2 management development. At a personal rather than a cool analytical level, individuals recognize that they need to learn something. Such experiences can be described as 'triggers'.

Managers will tend to think of managerial activities and problems first, and only recognize a learning need as a secondary requirement, and stage, in their thought processes. It is significant and sometimes hurtful experiences, or being faced with something new, or being exposed to a different kind of activity or a different boss, which helps to stimulate the recognition that learning has occurred, or could occur in a similar situation.

One way of using the Type 2 approach, or at least encouraging it among line managers, is to ask them to consider the opportunities that exist for learning from real management work. Figure 6.1 (which has already appeared on page 3) can create such a review, often interestingly without using the word 'need' at all. Managers can be helped to consider opportunities for learning which from our point of view include an implicit recognition of needs without actually being explicitly exposed to the word or concept 'need'.

Figure 6.1 Learning Opportunities

The opportunities identified here are not necessarily separate. You may, for example, think of something first in terms of something happening at a meeting – or you may think of the way in which one of your colleagues achieved success at a meeting.

Situations within the organization
Meetings
Task – familiar
    – unfamiliar
Task force
Customer visit
Visit to plant/office
Managing a change
Social occasions
Foreign travel
Acquisitions/mergers
Closing something down

Situations outside your organization
Charity
Domestic life
Industry committee
Professional meetings
Sports club

Processes
Coaching
Counselling
Listening
Modelling
Problem solving
Observing
Questioning
Reading
Negotiating
Mentoring
Public speaking
Reviewing/auditing
Clarifying responsibilities
Walking the floor
Visioning
Strategic planning
Problem diagnosis
Decision making
Selling

People
Boss
Mentor
Network contacts
Peers
Consultants
Subordinates

The reader may like to consider how to take advantage of these various approaches to identify need from the perspective of business reality indicated here.

1   Do we currently have a business plan which could be used in the ways indicated here?

2   If we do not have a business plan is there some other process of discussing major objectives for my unit in which I could be involved and from which I could help to generate management development needs?

3   What is the balance between formal analysis via skills or competencies and the kind of 'felt hurt' approach in my organization at present?

4   How can I relate the suggestions on Type 1 and Type 2 processes to the identification of needs?

THE IMPACT OF ORGANIZATIONAL CULTURE

Since reference has frequently been made in this book to the contingent nature of management, and the fact that different organizations will need and respond to different processes, it will be no surprise that the culture of the organization influences assessment of needs in at least two different ways. One of the purposes of management development can actually be to change that organizational culture.

The nature of the organization can determine the kind of management development which is appropriate or acceptable. This point could have been made in the previous chapter on systems, but has been included here because it probably has its most direct expression in terms of the dual aspect of needs:

● what an organization wants to achieve in terms of improved or changed skills
● what processes it might choose in order to determine those needs

Handy[20] argues that some organizational cultures are better fitted for what we would call formal management development systems, or for particular elements in those systems. The suggestions here about using and developing from Type 1 to Type 2 in our model may, for instance, be more acceptable to organizational cultures which emphasize task and person rather than those Handy identifies as power cultures or role cultures. The particularities of the impact of an organization's culture on what the needs are and how they should be identified is illustrated implicitly rather than explicitly in the articles on AIB, Ford and British Airways. Some aspects of needs in a single but changing organizational culture (building societies) are given in the article by Smith.[21]

DO ENTREPRENEURIAL MANAGERS HAVE DIFFERENT NEEDS?

One of the problems here is to establish exactly what form of entrepreneurship is being discussed. Is it the entrepreneur running a small organization from scratch of perhaps fifty people, or is it the successful entrepreneur who has moved on to run a more substantial business, like Anita Roddick of Body Shop or Steve Shirley of F International, or is it indeed the entrepreneur like Clive Sinclair, apparently unable to sustain early success? Some of the characteristics said to distinguish the entrepreneur from the 'normal' manager clearly relate to issues of size rather than entrepreneurship: one example is the need to be effective in close contact with both customers and employees at a personal level. Entrepreneurs may well need this skill; but so do managers of small companies who are in no sense entrepreneurs.

It may well be that entrepreneurial organizations have particular needs, but it is just as dangerous to generalize about these as it is about any form of organization. The skills involved in creativity would generally be thought to be peculiarly appropriate to entrepreneurial organizations; yet creativity in business can lead to unsuccessful answers at least as often as it leads to good ones.

INNOVATION AND CHANGE

A more useful dimension than the pure entrepreneurial issue is that of the different managerial skills associated with innovation. Here we have the advantage of the literally masterly book by Kanter.[22] The new skills required in securing successful change apply to a much wider variety of organizations than those which could be defined as entrepreneurial. These are:

- power skills – persuading others to invest information and support resources in new initiatives
- skills in managing problems associated with greater use of teams
- understanding how change is designed and constructed in an organization

One of the most useful aspects of Kanter's book is the reminder it offers that skills will not develop successfully without an appropriate facilitating context. Her emphasis on the nature of the innovative organization is a reminder that innovative skills can be neither successfully identified nor developed in isolation from the organizational context.

THE LEARNING ORGANIZATION

Organizations, like individuals, have to change and adapt to meet new circumstances. The processes necessary to measure the changes required are no different from those we have already discussed. An organization which takes learning seriously may pursue any learning processes with a greater level of intensity. It may be that a strong push to change the culture might entitle an organization to be called 'a learning organization'. I do not think that research so far has shown that the processes of establishing these needs are any different from those set out in this chapter.

REFERENCES

1 MUMFORD A. 'Counselling senior managers' development'. In BOYDELL T. and PEDLER M. (eds.). *Management self development*. Gower, 1981

2 ROSE D. 'Management development in the Thomson Organisation'. In MUMFORD A. *Handbook of management development*. Gower, 1991

3 CUNNINGHAM I. and LEON P. 'Focusing management development'. *Journal of European Industrial Training*. Vol 10, No 8, 1986

4 STEWART A. 'Diagnosing needs'. In MUMFORD A. *Handbook of management development*. Gower, 1991

5 PEDLER M., BURGOYNE J. and BOYDELL T. *A manager's guide to self development*. 2nd ed. McGraw Hill, 1986

6 BOYATZIS R. *The competent manager*. John Wiley, 1982

7 BURGOYNE J. 'Competency approaches to management development'. *Transition*, February 1989.

8 HIRSH W. *What makes a manager*. Institute of Manpower Studies, 1988

9 STEWART R. *Contrast in management*. McGraw Hill, 1975

10 MINTZBERG H. *The value of managerial work*. Prentice Hall, 1980

11 KOTTER J. P. *The general manager*. Free Press, 1982

12 MINTZBERG H. 'The manager's job: folklore and fact'. *Harvard Business Review*, July/August 1975

13 KOTTER J. 'What effective general managers really do'. *Harvard Business Review*, November/December 1982

14 MUMFORD A. 'What managers really do'. *Management Decision.* Vol 26, No 5, 1988
15 MUMFORD A. *Developing top managers.* Gower, 1988
16 BENNIS W. *Leaders.* Harper and Row, 1985
17 KOTTER J. P. *The leadership factor.* Free Press, 1988
18 BRUCE M. 'Managing people first'. *Industrial and Commercial Training.* March 1987
19 SEEKINGS, D. and WILSON B. 'Allied Irish Bank in Britain: organisational and business development through action learning'. *Business Education.* Vol 9, No 3, 1988
20 HANDY C. *Understanding organizations.* Penguin, 1985
21 SMITH D. 'Organisational culture and management development in building societies'. *Personnel Review.* Vol 15, No 3, 1986
22 KANTER R. *The change masters.* Simon and Schuster, 1983

7 Formal Processes for Development on the Job

Chapter 4 described the systems of formal management development set up to overcome the major disadvantages of relying on accidental learning for the development of managers. The achieved learning that resulted from such systems was described there in terms of the effectiveness of the system as a system: whether job moves were actually planned and achieved, whether courses achieved some recognizable result. When we move beyond the system to the particular processes involved in implementing the systematic plans, we are faced with a dilemma.

Type 3 formal management development characteristically provides for someone to be moved into a new job, to work in a different country or on a different product, or to work for a different boss and with different colleagues. It does so because without formal planning and direction, accidental opportunities will be insufficient. Yet what happens as a result of the Type 3 initiative is that managers are actually largely placed in Type 1 learning contexts: in many organizations no attempt is made to improve the effectiveness of the learning and development process within the new job.

It is in this situation that the difficulty of judgement arises. Do we look at this with an amused smile and treat it as a characteristically British oddity? Do we argue that formal management development processes in effect stop at the manager's door, thereafter relying on initiative and drive to secure self-development? Or do we see the situation as an area of inefficiency that can be corrected?

The contention of this book is that once we have seen that the Emperor has no clothes we must look for some. It is unnecessary and intolerable that we remain aloof from the reality of how

116

managers do and could learn from opportunities on the job. We need to provide help to managers on how to learn more effectively.

Not the least benefit of doing this, from the point of view of formal management development, would be that improved learning productivity from planned, on-the-job opportunities would increase the credibility of the formal scheme. Not only would individual managers benefit from an improved capacity to take advantage of the opportunities provided by the scheme, but in doing so they would be more likely to recognize that the scheme has actually produced these beneficial results.

A major cause of failures in this area has been the grotesque lack of attention paid to learning processes in institutions which provide off-the-job learning. If individuals are not helped to develop their learning processes in those circumstances uniquely dedicated to learning, it is not surprising that little is done on the job to encourage understanding of learning processes. The essential features of the learning process are discussed in greater detail in Chapter 11, but for our immediate purposes we need to recognize that:

- learning is not a single achieved/not achieved process, but one involving different stages of learning with different achievements (the concept of the learning cycle)
- different individuals may respond better or worse, and be able to deal more or less effectively, with different stages of the cycle. Thus the concept of individual learning preferences expressed as learning styles.

PLANS FOR DEVELOPMENT

Although learning is something that can be achieved only by the learner (i.e. it cannot be achieved by a teacher), in most managerial contexts and for most managerial purposes it is also a social activity. For managers it is often an activity with organizational purpose, drives and rewards. So the individual manager may be 'driven' towards learning through a formal appraisal. That may lead to a personal development plan which sets out what the individual intends to achieve and what the organization will do to aid achievement. The idea now increasingly suggested is that of a 'learning contract' between the individual and the organization. My preference is for the term 'learning agreement'. In terms of normal working relationships between a manager and subordinates the term 'contract' is unrealistic. It is difficult to envisage them in their normal day-to-day dealings thinking or writing to each other in these terms whereas agreements are put into effect, though not necessarily on paper, all the time in the course of their managerial work.

Figure 7.1 lists the 'planned and deliberate learning processes' which have already been set out in more detail on pages 11–12.

Figure 7.1   Planned and Deliberate Learning Processes

Changes in job
- promotion
- same job but in different function or product: job rotation
- secondment

Changes in job content
- stretching boundaries of job by extra responsibility and tasks
- special projects
- committees or task groups
- junior boards

Within the job
- coaching
- counselling
- monitoring and feedback by boss
- mentoring

CHANGES IN JOB

There are significant differences in the nature of the opportunities provided by different types of change and of the difficulties involved in taking up the opportunities. The levels of difficulty were indicated in Figure 3.3 (see page 62).

Moving into a New Job

Whether the move is planned by the manager's current employer, or whether a new organization takes the arriving manager on, the same development issues arise. What is the new manager to learn, at what pace and through what processes?

As Figure 3.3 indicates, the most difficult move of all, yet the one with the most potential learning, is promotion into a new organization. Some kind of induction programme will usually be arranged. The new manager will meet new colleagues, will probably be given a tour of the office and perhaps of other working facilities.

There may be arrangements to meet a range of customers, suppliers and other useful contacts. In essence the manager has to learn about the nature and purpose of the organization – 'getting to know the business'. Then there is the need to find out about internal relationships: the politics of the business, the way in which people work together, or avoid working together. Finally there is the outside world, the people and organizations serviced.

Rosemary Stewart[1] points out that acquiring the *knowledge* necessary to perform a new job is relatively unstressful. It is more difficult for the manager to understand and respond to differences in the *managerial processes* in the job. She provides a useful checklist on the nature of these differences.

> **Example**
> A newly appointed general manager of an overseas subsidiary of a UK multinational was brought to the UK for a week. His programme included a number of visits to different people at Head Office, Research Division, several managers of similar companies. The original design of the programme filled almost the whole of the week with visits and travel, with no opportunity for the manager to review what he had learned and to check out that he had learned appropriately. Two review sessions were therefore built in, during which he reviewed what he had learned from his visits and contacts with his immediate boss and the main Board Director concerned.

Gabarro[2] describes in a most helpful article the stages involved when managers move into a new job:

- taking hold
- immersion
- reshaping
- consolidation
- refinement

The example above shows that effective action can be taken to help with the stage Gabarro describes as 'taking hold'. Gabarro sets out the further requirements for this stage:

- make sure priorities are set out for the new manager
- provide processes by which new managers work out expectations with their new subordinates

- give support in areas of lack of knowledge or experience
- accept that taking charge takes time

Gabarro says that short-term assignments – by which he means appointment to a full job but for a short period – are not likely to be successful. He derives this view from the research which established the five stages described above, which he found took from two to two and a half years. My own experience would support his view that without a substantial period of this kind it is not possible for most managers in most jobs to learn how to do the new job effectively. What some of them can do successfully is demonstrate that they can analyse problems and requirements well and set in motion processes of improvement. If they are moved on after a year or eighteen months, they not only all too often fail to learn in depth from what they have done so far, but the relatively short period of implementation means that they may actually have received incorrect feedback about the accuracy of their analyses. The organization may also make a wrong judgement about the effectiveness of the manager involved.

What is involved here is clearer recognition that the transition between jobs, whether promotion or movement sideways, involves a great deal more than some prior training and development activities and an initial induction period. This transition frequently provides only informal and accidental learning. In part this is because of failure by formal management development processes and organizers to recognize exactly what is involved in these transitions and to provide formal development plans during the transition. It is not simply a case of waiting for the first review of the manager's performance (probably a formal appraisal) and picking out from it the learning needs that experience on the job has identified. It is quite possible to see in advance what at least some of those learning needs will be and to plan for them formally. The review would then more usefully be of both performance and the achievement of and learning from that experience. Of course those converted to the ideas of this book will also want to encourage Type 2 learning both by initial discussions with the participants and perhaps by suggesting that powerful incidents are reviewed by the managers involved from time to time.

To summarize, moving to a new job creates learning opportunities but does not satisfy them in a 'planned and deliberate way'. The special learning opportunities arising from the new appointment merge gradually into opportunities arising within a job which is no longer recognizably new.

Secondment

I define secondment as a process of moving a manager into a job outside his employing organization. Some organizations and writers have taken a rather broader view, so that secondment actually includes moving people across divisions or from one company to another within a group of companies. While some of the motivation for either kind of secondment move may well be the same – to provide a job for a manager – the development processes involved are likely to be considerably different. So it is more sensible to regard movement within an employing organization when undertaken within a formal development scheme as a form of job rotation. Of course there are organizations where relationships between the different parts of a group are so tenuous that in practice the same novelty pertains!

This discussion is concerned with secondment as a development process, and not with secondment as a means of finding a possibly temporary job for a manager who would otherwise be redundant, or who is out of favour with his or her superiors. The secondment may in certain instances have a dual learning objective. For example, secondment of a manager from industry to work in the Civil Service normally has a double objective; the individual learns from exposure to a different culture, a different environment, a different way of doing things. At a secondary level the organization sponsoring the secondee learns about how the Civil Service operates and may therefore learn how to deal with it more effectively. Indeed, there may be a very precise relationship between secondment from industry to, say, the Department of Trade and Industry and the acquisition of knowledge about the process the department goes through in considering particular issues.

As the IPM code on secondment says,[3] it provides a 'unique development opportunity for employees to learn to perform in challenging new situations'. The code also says that 'the secondee must be debriefed to elicit what has been learned from the secondment'. Secondment may involve the acquisition of particular areas of knowledge, or the generation of particular types of experience. There are benefits to be derived from transfer to a quite different country, which may offer an experience not otherwise available within the organization.

One of the main benefits to many of the companies who engaged in secondment during the 1980s was that of exposing a manager to a quite different sort of experience in terms of 'standing on their own feet'. Several large organizations told me that many of their managers had been brought up in an environment in which they had a great deal of professional and functional support in carrying out their jobs – sometimes perhaps more than they really wanted. To go to a small organization where they had to do everything for themselves was thought to be a considerable development opportunity.

As this point illustrates, different kinds of secondment have different objectives. Civil Service type secondment really involves the acquisition of knowledge, whereas secondment from a large to a small company gives a different kind of experience and probably an opportunity to develop different kinds of skills. As much as anything, however, these latter secondments are about responsibility, authority and the application, perhaps, of some management knowledge not fully utilized in the sponsoring organization.

The emphasis here is on the development benefit to the individual and to the sponsoring organization. The prime objective of some secondments is obviously different. Secondment can be a way of getting rid of someone for a time; but it can, more generously, be the result of a decision by an organization to put something into the community concerned. This happens when organizations send somebody to work for a charity, perhaps through the work of the Action Resource Centre. Although there are glowing exceptions, research by the Centre for Employment Initiatives found that this form of secondment was not usually undertaken as a method of career development, although organizations sometimes claimed it as such. Most often the people seconded were either nearing retirement or for one reason or another 'available'. In these latter cases, of course, the end result of the secondment may have been to send back a manager who was actually better equipped or happier than when he left; but that seems not to have been the prime purpose or the stimulus for any planned development within the secondment.

The nature of secondment is obscured by dramatic examples of high-flying managers seconded, for example, from industry to the public sector. In recent years perhaps the two best known examples were the secondment of Sir Michael Edwardes from Chloride to what was then British Leyland, and Len Peach from IBM to the National Health Service.

FERTILIZATION WITHIN THE JOB

Movement between jobs at the same level is job rotation. The idea is that just as an agricultural crop will extract all the goodness from one location and therefore benefit by being grown in a different one, so with managers. The agricultural analogy can be developed further by considering development opportunities within existing jobs. Instead of being moved to a different location to get development benefit, the manager can extract more from the existing location. Formal management development does this by identifying particular kinds of work that can be available within and around the existing job. Again, all too often opportunities are provided without any effective development taking place. The formal process is only properly effective when the job is actually fertilized, rather than treated as naturally fertile ground from which useful things will grow. The fertilization involves the construction of effective learning and development processes around the opportunities provided. We will now look at some examples of opportunities.

Stretching Boundaries and Acquiring New Tasks

This is the process by which a manager, without changing job title, is given additional responsibilities or a greater weight of responsibility. An example of this would be that of a sales director handing over to a sales manager responsibility for a major national account previously handled by the director. Another would be delegating to a subordinate manager the task of producing a report, visiting an important customer or negotiating with a trades union.

Committees/Working Parties/Task Forces

Line executives most frequently assign managers to special committees or task forces for purely managerial reasons. The group wants a particular expert on the subject or a representative from a particular area in the business or somebody who is known to have the ear of somebody important. Such appointments may lead to Type 1 learning.

However, the responsible executive may actually consider the development opportunity involved, either because he has a personal interest or because the personnel director or management development adviser suggests it. If this is not discussed between the line executive and the appointed manager, then the manager will not be aware that his career has been influenced by formal processes. Where someone is appointed for development reasons it is much more desirable to discuss those reasons and identify the development opportunities and ways of benefiting from them. These opportunities may arise from the exposure of a manager to a quite different process, or to a different level of management, or they may give the manager the opportunity of acquiring functional knowledge. The opportunity may also involve the development of skills, such as managing meetings, or the more subtle skills of influencing others (sometimes pejoratively called political skills).

Junior Boards

Managers can stay in their existing jobs but be given experience in simulating the processes of their board of directors. They may be given the same information as the board on a particular issue. They may be asked to consider it and make recommendations to the board, perhaps against criteria which the board has set. Such 'junior boards' have obviously been set up with primarily development objectives. Perhaps because they are so purely developmental they have not really been widely accepted. The main reason seems to be that their actual lack of responsibility and accountability means that the discussions are frustratingly lacking in identifiable results. The knowledge acquired, either in terms of the content of the managerial decisions required or of the process, seems to be outweighed by feelings of psychological and managerial impotence.

Visits to Customers, Suppliers and Others

A production director was identified through the company's resource plan as having high potential for promotion to a general manager position. It was recognized, however, that he had had experience in only two of the functions (production and supply) for which he was likely later to carry overall responsibility. A personal development plan, produced in discussion with him, identified two courses of action (among a larger number not repeated here). The first was to remedy the fact that his experience had all been focused within the plant. It was arranged he would accompany two sales managers over a period of five or six weeks. On his return he said

> As a production director I had always thought that sales made life difficult for us. It took these visits to show

me exactly how the customer makes life difficult for them. It also really brought home to me that if you cannot satisfy the customer (and on some of the visits we could not), you did not sell, and if you do not sell there is nothing for production actually to have to moan about!

As a further step this individual was appointed to a working party on the development of a new product, through which he was exposed to a great deal of marketing analysis and marketing strategy. (As a final comment it is interesting to note that this particular individual declined the opportunity to go on a general management course, on the grounds that he preferred to learn in the ways indicated here.)

Other examples include a sales director who was given the experience of observing a production line; he became much more sympathetic to the problems facing a production director trying to cope with short runs rather than economical long runs. A senior manager in a growing company which had good and informally based relations with its employees recognized that it would need to review these processes and perhaps to change them. It identified a manager not currently in the personnel function to go and find out what other comparable companies did. His visits were seen both as acquiring knowledge for the company and about developing the understanding he had of appropriate practices for which it was envisaged he might be given special responsibility.

Projects and On-the-job Development

Projects can be a development tool in all the processes mentioned so far. The manager in a new job can take up a major project as a development process, for example 'find out why repeat orders have declined by 28 per cent in the last six months'. A secondment can include a project or indeed be totally dedicated to one. 'We are seconding you to charity X for six months. Your Project is to review their management control systems, and produce a report for the Chairman of their council.' Projects can also be identified within the existing job. 'We want you to do an investigation into the forecasts actually used by sales, marketing and production. Why do they have different forecasts and what problems result?'

It will be clear from the abbreviated terms of reference that any of these projects could have been set up as purely managerial exercises, resulting at best in informal learning – Type 1. They were actually Type 3 development opportunities, because the manager selected to carry them out was chosen for development reasons as well as for managerial. There was also discussion with the individual about why he had been given the project as a development exercise. This was supplemented by a relatively short but effective discussion on how the manager might take the best advantage of the development opportunity. In each case a development plan was agreed and in both cases a short review session was held at the end of the project, separate from the managerial project presentation and review.

Projects provide major potential developmental benefits. They often involve managers in looking at a wider range of issues, in greater depth, across a wider range of functions than might otherwise be encountered. At their best, even within a formal development context, projects of the kind described here should be real rather than invented purely for development. In some cases they carry responsibility for implementation as well as recommendation, in which case they provide for the strongest form of development. Even projects in which the participant does not carry final responsibility can, if properly managed from a development point of view, provide good learning.

Projects have increasingly been recognized in the Management Development world as powerful and useful development aids. They have the great advantage of being definable and separable pieces of managerial work with a beginning and an end. The development opportunities and components can be clearly identified, while at the same time they are seen by managers as real managerial tasks with identifiable managerial benefits.

However, simply providing a process through which project opportunities are created for managers is not fully effective Type 3 management development. Unless the development opportunities are analysed, discussed and the actual processes of learning are understood and employed by the manager involved, the learning is still accidental rather than planned and deliberate learning.

The concept of action learning – learning from real managerial work on real managerial problems – includes projects as a major vehicle (see Chapter 2). It is not, however, simply 'learning by doing'. The doing element is a necessary but not a sufficient requirement. Action learning involves doing through a designed and organized approach which is explicitly intended to incorporate learning as well as managing. In its best form action learning is the prime example of effective learning from projects. Any project

potentially involves learning: but this may be informal and accidental. The action learning process deliberately aims to secure learning
through a defined process: 'what have we learned from and with
each other?'

A project may therefore be stimulated by the management
development process as a purely individual activity involving
individual reflection and subsequent discussion of learning achieved.
In its action learning version it involves a wider group of people,
perhaps discussing a number of projects, and certainly stimulating
and fertilizing each other with different ideas, different problems
and different solutions. Action learning has blurred the distinctions
between on-the-job and off-the-job development, which is part of
the explanation for its usefulness and success.

Readers may like to return to their answers to the exercises
given in Chapter 1 on the processes used in their own organization
for on-the-job development.

Exercise

1 As a result of reading this chapter so far, do you see any ways
   in which you could make use of some processes you do not
   currently use?
2 Do you see ways of improving your use of the processes you do
   currently use?
3 In what ways does your organization currently assist managers
   to learn from the opportunities created for them through the
   formal scheme? Could this be improved?
4 Which of the processes outlined in this chapter have been the
   most powerful and useful in your organization? Why?

LEARNING WITHIN THE JOB

In this section we are concerned with the ways in which learning
is assisted, as distinct from the previous section which reviewed
opportunities.

Coaching

In the 1970s, coaching was seen as the up-and-coming management
development tool. Singer[4] wrote a complete book about it, and
Moorby[5] provided explicit guidance. Since then very little seems

to have been written about it, and there are few indications that
the subject appears in those formal courses where we might expect
it to appear. Part of the reason may be some uncertainty about
what the word actually means. Moorby's first article[6] said that
'managers mostly carry out coaching as and when opportunities
occur by responding to situations'; but he did not then define what
coaching is. In his second article[7] he says that it is 'taking the
problems, opportunities, and frustrations of the job itself and using
them constructively to improve the skills, the knowledge and the
performance of managers'. Singer says it is 'concerned more with
asking questions which help a man to think than with teaching him
what to do'. Singer tried to draw a distinction between coaching
and counselling. He saw counselling as direct help to an individual,
whereas he envisaged coaching as a joint process in which 'the
coach is as likely to learn as much as is the person he is coaching'.
Megginson and Boydell[8] do not go as far as this. They describe
coaching as 'a process in which a manager, through direct discussion
and guided activity, helps a colleague to solve a problem or to do
a task better than would otherwise have been the case'.

The problem all of these authors sought to overcome was that
coaching, in the normally understood sense, involves a much more
direct process of instruction. While their emphasis is undoubtedly
the most important one from a development point of view – since
it reconfirms the point about people learning only what they are
willing to learn – they are perhaps too exclusive. There are situations
in which an individual can and should be taken through an organized
process of being told what it is necessary to do before doing it.
(Admittedly in a managerial context these will be the minority of
cases.) When managers do this they are getting close to being a
teacher or instructor.

One of the issues is that the manager as coach primarily wants
the task done well and only secondarily wants the individual to
learn from doing it. As a third factor he or she may also want the
individual to learn from the process of discussing the task. It is not
surprising that ordinary human beings do not always manage to
achieve all three objectives with the appropriate degree of balance.

Nor is it surprising that our normal human beings vary in
both their capacity as managers to apply coaching and as people to
receive it. The reflective listening, analytical, objective coaching
style is far removed from the normal style of many managers and
it is not surprising that many of them find it difficult to employ. It
may well be that one of the reasons why coaching seems to have
disappeared as a prime component of the new wave of management

development is that the managerial style required to do it effectively is too antipathetic to too many managers. Further complications arise from the preferred learning styles of both the coach and the person being coached. In terms of the Honey/Mumford learning styles, to require an Activist boss to be a reflective listening coach to an Activist subordinate is a recipe for failure. If there is mutual understanding there is a slightly greater chance of success with an Activist boss and a Reflector subordinate, if they have actually exchanged views about the learning process involved and their own separate learning styles. On the other hand, Reflector boss and a Reflector subordinate may well enjoy and benefit from the kind of coaching described in the literature.

The prescription for creating an effective coaching relationship within a formal management development system is relatively clear. It is not only necessary to assist managers to develop the skills involved in coaching, such as effective listening, observation, giving non-evaluative feedback. It is also necessary to help the coach and the subordinate understand the learning processes involved in the act of coaching.

Counselling

While Singer's attempt to separate counselling and coaching is understandable, the fact is that in many management development systems the processes are confused – probably because they are in fact, difficult to separate. Counselling may clearly be taking place when a manager discusses issues of domestic significance and difficulty with a subordinate. It may still be counselling when the discussion centres on problems with personal relationships at work. But is it counselling or coaching if the discussion focuses on how the subordinate's aggressive instincts towards the head of another department can be reduced to a level acceptable to both sides? A discussion about an individual's career may also be counselling. 'Everything about the way you do your job tells me that you are much happer giving advice than having to scurry round implementing actions. I think your next job should be in staff function and not in the line.' But suppose the guidance is offered differently. 'What do you think about the way you responded to the need to fight a number of fires last week? Looking back, do you think you might have behaved differently? What were the causes of the ways in which you did behave? What were the things that influenced you?' Is this the launching pad for a counselling discussion on future career, or is it the beginning of a coaching discussion about how a manager should improve his reaction to certain kinds of event?

The extremes of coaching and counselling are distinguishable, yet both of them require rather similar skills in areas of common interest. Some managers will be able to make direct statements under either coaching or counselling umbrellas, while being able to carry out a more gentle non-evaluative process under either heading.

Indeed, the whole problem of these distinct management development processes of coaching and counselling is that managers do not readily key into them. They are seen as formal management development processes which have no direct association with what happens in real life. Most managers do not see themselves as coaches or counsellors. They deal with business issues, with management problems and management activities. They provide guidance and help on these. If management development advisers choose to call the process by which the help is offered 'coaching' well, with a politely resigned shrug, so be it. When I pointed out to a manager I worked with a few years ago the 'coaching' aspects of his normal behaviour, the light dawned. 'You mean if I am helping somebody with a problem, without telling him what the answer is, that's coaching. If you want to call it that, OK. I call it helping him with his problem.' Yet again we face the issue that all too often formal management development processes are seen by the managers they are intended to help as separate from the world in which they live. The designation I would really prefer is 'mutual problem solving'. That covers the reality of a normal managerial working relationship between boss and subordinate. That is why it appears as a Type 1 and Type 2 process rather than as a Type 3 process. Perhaps in five or ten years a later edition of this book will be able to include it in this chapter.

It is very necessary to put over the basic idea of the coaching concept to managers. They would otherwise concern themselves exclusively with improving task performance, whereas they need to draw out with subordinates, through explicit learning review, how to build on that performance.

Mentoring
Clutterbuck[9] says that this was an unknown term until the late 1970s. He may well be right about its application within formal management development systems, but the essential informal process was certainly well known in management, as in other aspects of life. As a formal process it was first implemented in the

United States and most of the research and literature still comes from there, although Clutterbuck's book provides additional UK material.

The idea of an older manager choosing a younger manager for whom he will act as coach, counsellor or sponsor is one that has long existed informally and accidentally. The process of nurturing the growth of another individual as a planned input within a formal scheme is newer. One of the problems with this word, as with so many others, is that organizations and authors define it differently. Most of the American literature includes the manager's direct boss as a mentor. This confuses two roles. Chapter 9 indicates the variety of roles carried out by the boss; but they are carried out precisely because the boss is managerially responsible for someone else. It is much more helpful to restrict the term mentor to someone who has no direct responsibility: usually someone older, probably from another department or another division, or even from outside the manager's own organization.

Even within that more restrictive definition there are different aspects of the role, and different ways of carrying it out. Some mentors are 'door openers': they try and ensure that their protégés are considered for important jobs, assignments, projects. They ensure that those who make decisions about people know what their protégé has achieved, and why that level of achievement is noteworthy. The door–opening role is rather that of a sponsor; and of course the protégé may not be aware of it. How pleasant for the mentor to be able to murmur in later years that he created the opening for someone who has subsequently shot upwards in the organization! Formal management development schemes do, however, make the relationship explicit, turning it from an informal into a formal management development process.

The other major type of mentor relationship is one in which a more experienced manager 'coaches' a less experienced one via discussions about work issues, job performance, politics and relationships. This offers more opportunity of facilitating the less experienced manager's learning, because the process is explicit. This can be especially helpful in encouraging the development of women managers. (There are, of course, very few examples of women acting as mentors of men.)

Mentoring is a highly personal relationship, which can some-times lead to a level of dependence. Because of the potential benefits, but also the potential problems, some organizations have run formal programmes in training both mentors and protégés. These can certainly be helpful in defining expectations at both an organizational and an individual level and can take on board such problems as whether the senior male and junior female manager relationship – which can be effective in facilitating promotion – is none the less potentially harmful in its reinforcement of male/female stereotypes.

As with the other processes, the styles of mentor and the protégé need to be compatible for the protégé to actually learn from the relationship.

Modelling on boss, colleagues, outsiders

Some managers learn by observing others. The modelling may be positive – seeing someone doing something well and doing it that way yourself. Or it may be negative – seeing something done with disastrous results and deciding to give that technique or process a miss. Most frequently this is a Type 1 experience; but sometimes the formal system provides the opportunity. Formal management development ought to include help on how to observe others at work, and how to build in review processes after the observation.

Acquiring feedback

We have fortunately long passed the stage of accepting in a management development policy that a 'manager is responsible for developing his or her subordinates'. We have recognized that no one can be 'responsible' for the development of anyone else: the boss has a role in helping the development of subordinates. In the Type 3 context it is the job of the boss to monitor and give feedback on performance. (Colleagues give informal feedback.) This is required primarily for effective performance but is also essential to learning and development. Most management development systems concentrate on improving the validity of the performance review and pay very little attention to the reviewing of learning and development. The role of the boss is so fundamental that it requires more extended discussion, which occurs in Chapter 9.

Reading

Managers read a great deal; but they usually read technical, professional or industrial material connected with their work. In the United Kingdom, at any rate, they read books and articles on management less frequently. Yet articles are circulated, particularly among senior managers, 'for your interest', sometimes by the chief executive and sometimes the personnel director. Managers buy and quite often read at least part of the best sellers like *In search of excellence* or *Iacocca*. The formal scheme ought to integrate this kind of relatively casual reading into the planned development of individuals. This could be done by suggesting discussion meetings, or better still by recommending that time is set aside at normal management meetings. In my research I came across a number of organizations where copies of *In search of excellence* had been circulated, presumably because the person responsible thought that his or her colleagues could learn from it. Yet, oddly, the book had never been discussed.

THE QUALITY OF ACHIEVEMENT

The emphasis throughout this chapter has been that management development systems have been characterized more by their attempt to provide opportunities for learning on the job than by attempts to improve the quality of such learning. It therefore becomes additionally difficult to define achievement in this area. If the opportunity has been provided but has not been taken up, then whose is the failure? Since the attempt is being made under a Type 3 banner, the failure actually lies within the formal management development scheme. Until we clarify our objectives to include actually helping with the process rather than simply providing the opportunity, then the level of achievement in relation to any particular opportunity will be no different from the lack of achievement on the equivalent opportunity provided by informal and accidental processes. The formal scheme may have increased the number and range of opportunities; but it will not have increased the capacity of the manager to take advantage of them.

The need is therefore primarily to design in additional quality by increasing the content of the formal processes. The scattered, accidental, occasionally bruising nature of the learning process which occurs in normal, informal managerial work may be acceptable because no one is pretending that the process is other than a byproduct. When we start improving development through formal processes, we cannot afford to stop providing informal opportunities; these focus the very process which we want to improve – the ability to learn.

Methods for improving the quality of the learning process, in both Type 2 and Type 3 modes, are provided in Chapter 11. They are taken together, because of course the attention to learning and development processes recommended here for Type 3 purposes will have the great virtue of enabling managers to improve their capacity for accidental learning from experiences, converting them into Type 2.

Exercise

1 What steps have we taken to assist in formally providing opportunities for development on the job?
2 What steps have we taken to assist managers to take advantage of these opportunities, and to assist their bosses to make them more meaningful in the provision of effective learning?
3 How many of these opportunities do we in fact provide? Are there some which we do not currently use which could be suggested to some or all of our managers?
4 What steps could be taken to help on issues such as coaching and mentoring?

REFERENCES

1 STEWART R. 'Developing managers by radical job moves'. *Journal of Management Development*. Vol 3, No 2, 1984
2 GABARRO J. 'When a new manager takes charge'. *Harvard Business Review*. May–June 1985
3 IPM. *IPM Secondment Code*. Institute of Personnel Management, 1988
4 SINGER E. J. *Effective management coaching*. Institute of Personnel Management, 1979
5 MOORBY E. 'The manager as coach'. *Personnel Management*. November 1973
6 *ibid*
7 MOORBY E. 'Coaching in context'. *Personnel Management*. November 1975
8 MEGGINSON D. and BOYDELL T. *A manager's guide to coaching*. BACIE, 1979
9 CLUTTERBUCK D. *Everybody needs a mentor*. Institute of Personnel Management, 1985

8 Planned Development off the Job

The problem with development processes centred on the job is that their great strength – reality – constantly poses the risk of seduction. The manager's attention is always likely to be seduced by the reality and felt priority of the managerial activity involved away from focusing on learning.

The case for taking managers away from that reality and putting them on a course is precisely that they are then able to concentrate entirely on learning rather than managing. Nor is it only a question of focus of attention. Informal managerial learning through normal work practices is insufficient, inefficient and dangerous. But even the improved Type 2 version of learning through real work is unlikely to produce a manager fully capable of operating effectively in the modern world. Although we can greatly increase the productivity of learning through real-life experiences, they will still offer learning only within the limits of those experiences. You cannot learn on the job anything which is not available within or around it. You cannot develop a skill if that skill is not actually employed currently. An even more pervasive problem is that you cannot improve your level of skill if there is no one else around capable of demonstrating coaching or facilitating your development of it.

Two examples will help to illustrate. Most managers learn how to conduct selection interviews through 'informal and accidental' processes; they have some experience of being interviewed, they carry out interviews themselves and they may have some discussions with other people about the process and the results they secure. These informal processes can certainly be improved by the application of the ideas given in Chapter 3. They can be improved further through an interviewing course. A well designed course will offer an appropriate balance of knowledge about the principles of interviewing, and practical exercises. Such a course is likely to include principles such as the interviewee's air time being quadruple that of the interviewer, and the need to ask open-ended questions. Those principles are carried into effect on the course by providing exercises in interviewing. Observations, video recording and skilled feedback will give the manager involved the chance to review the skills he has used and see how he might develop them further.

If we look at chairmanship we will see that the nature of the meetings managers chair varies according to their jobs, the organizations they are working in and the purpose of the particular activity. As with selection interviewing, the capacity to run meetings successfully can certainly be shown to develop from personal experience, and can be enhanced through improved learning on the job. A formal training course, if properly designed and delivered can develop through practice, observation, feedback and more practice the skills involved in running a meeting successfully rather than just 'chairing meetings'.

In each of these cases – deliberately chosen because they focus on common managerial activities – it is possible to see elements of knowledge and elements of skill. The knowledge could also be put over in writing – which is why there are popular books on management techniques. But the combination of knowledge and skill offered on a course designed to give the opportunity to work out the knowledge in practice makes for a much more effective learning process. It is the combination that makes the process effective, and which may also bring into play a third element: attitude.

It is possible that attitudes, which are inevitably learned informally, can be changed via a more considered learning process on the job. But a well designed course can achieve attitude change more effectively, through the combination of knowledge and skill reviewed through observation and feedback, which may generate new understanding and different attitudes. Whereas, for example, it is not unknown for a manager to be told that his or her attitude is wrong in the on-the-job situation, the influence of such a statement is often minimal. In a structured learning environment a manager who sees the results of his behaviour, either through a video or by feedback from colleagues, may be more motivated and better equipped to change.

We can take as an example one of the areas in which attitudes are most demonstrable and also very difficult to change. The male stereotype about female managers includes beliefs about their likelihood of continuing a managerial career or surrendering to domesticity, beliefs that women are emotional rather than rational, that they are soft rather than hard in their managerial dealings, and that other managers – 'although not me of course' – would have difficulty accepting a female boss. It would be proper to be modest in any claims about the influence that any course on women as managers, run for men, would have on these stereotypical attitudes. However, there is increasing evidence that whereas simply telling male managers that their attitude is wrong is ineffective, illustrating the nature and consequences of their stereotypical attitudes on a course shifts at least some managers some distance.

EFFECTIVENESS IS THE CORE

A manager is a person who gets things done. Some of those things are achieved by direct, personal and largely solitary activity; others are achieved by getting other people to do things. One of the problems in management training and education is that we tend to start by distinguishing knowledge, skill and attitude, as we did in the previous section. Yet managers do not characteristically think that way. They think about themselves and others in terms of relative effectiveness in getting things done. They may, through analysis of their success or failure, subsequently perceive a lack of knowledge, skill or attitudes. But they start from effectiveness: and effectiveness is defined by results actually secured not by knowledge or skill. To reiterate the point again, courses ought to work initially, if not always primarily, from what managers need to achieve.

Instead of giving emphasis to the provision of knowledge and asking managers to interpret and use that knowledge in subsequent action, we should give prime attention to action issues. This is more appropriate because it is actually about what managers do; it is also more successful because the managerial learner is more likely to be interested. Knowledge and the capacity to analyse and produce solutions to problems are necessary but insufficient contributors to effective action. Even attention to managerial skills, which looks at first sight a more attractive option, both to managers and to tutors, may be misplaced. The first focus of attention should be on the desired managerial result rather than on the particular skills required for achieving that result.

Some management trainers already do what I am suggesting. Others show that although they work on managerial skills, they do so on the basis of analysis of the particular skills and specific level of skill required in their organization (see Chapter 6). Others, in discussion, are slightly puzzled and say that since the analysis of skill requirements has already been undertaken it seems unduly long-winded to review them at the beginning of a programme, or to focus on issues of effectiveness first, when 'at the end of the day we are going to finish up with a list of skills that we knew they needed in the first place'.

It may indeed seem puzzling, if you have gone through the kind of careful analysis suggested in Chapters 4 and 6, that your first step in designing a course should be to put this analysis on one side. Yet this is a necessary step, both practically and psychologically. It is practically necessary for the reasons already suggested: managers will simply not attend to a discrete list of knowledge and skills in the way you would like or envisage.

The second reason is just as fundamental – and perhaps more difficult to accept. It is that management trainers and educators, for quite obvious and indeed quite admirable reasons, think they know a great deal more about the skills required for effective management than most managers. We have spent time reading about it, thinking about it, designing and redesigning courses on it. We finish up with an answer to which we are committed. In manufacturing industry that answer would be called a product. We become concerned to sell the product and deliver it successfully. All this is quite understandable, legitimate and, like many products, what we offer is – up to a point – very helpful to the customer. But the elaborate analysis of skills, knowledge and attitudes we have worked through may mean that the process we recommend is product rather than customer centred.

My own experience has been of successfully developing

Exercise

1 Go back to your answers to the questions in Chapter 6 about how you and your organization currently identify needs for improved skills or knowledge.
2 How do you use that analysis at the moment in designing courses?
3 What concepts about managerial skills, behaviours and effectiveness do you currently employ in the *design* of your courses (note the word design, not content)?
4 By what process do you currently try and engage the commitment of managers attending a course to what you will be doing on it, again focusing on issues of design not issues of nomination, preparation, design and preparation?

processes from the starting point that managers much prefer working from their understanding of management than from a textbook breakdown. This applies even to my modern gods of managerial behaviour – Stewart, Mintzberg and Kotter.

Readers may wish to test their own position against the views expressed in the first part of this chapter.

LINKAGES

Many of the suggestions here are linked with those in earlier chapters; there is a common theme of using managerial reality rather than ignoring it. It may be useful at this stage to summarize.

Managerial Reality

The focus for our development work ought to be reality not only because it is real, but because it engages the attention of managers. The problem with processes and content which do not engage and focus on reality is that for many managers they create learning problems rather than making learning easier and more effective.

Building on Experience

It is more sensible to build the design and content of formal training and education on the experience that managers have when they arrive on a course. It takes longer and may be less exciting for the tutor; but it is actually more effective.

Using Familiar Learning Processes

Although one of the great virtues of formal training and education is precisely that it focuses on learning rather than just doing, the achieved learning of managers will be low if the process is too different and distant from what managers usually do. Since managers do not customarily spend their time listening to lectures, even brilliantly delivered lecturers may not attract them. If they do not spend their time reviewing historical case studies of managerial practices in other organizations, a learning process based on this starts with some major disadvantages. Perhaps most powerfully of all, if the learning process, of whatever nature, is seen as something which is likely to be useful only on a course, not in real managerial life, then again our achievements will be more limited than they should be. We will have achieved something by causing managers to think in a different way, by giving them opportunities to listen, study, reflect and generate new ideas. But if they see these activities as applicable only in a formal course context, then we have limited our results.

Continued Learning

A follow-on from the last point is appropriate for many courses. It is desirable that the learner should continue learning after the course. This is not simply a matter of 'further reading' or individual action plans. These are partial but low level contributions. For any but short courses on particular techniques, participants should be given such an understanding of their own learning processes that they can seek out and use appropriate learning experiences beyond the confines of the course. A successful consequence of such attention would be a vast increase in Type 2 learning as a result of these Type 3 experiences. It is not necessary that all trainers and educators should use these particular descriptions; but it is desirable that they should take on board responsibility for enhancing the capacity of managers to learn outside as well as on their courses.

Preferred Approaches to Learning

Knowledge about what case studies or business games, lectures or role play can achieve is the grammar of our trade. It is our job to manipulate these basics to create meaning. But this meaning must be communicated to the receiving brain of a participant on a course. Different individuals have a different capacity to create sense from the same elements; they prefer their learning to be presented in

Figure 8.1   Manager-centred Learning

Managerial reality
Building on experience
Using familiar learning processes
Continued learning
Preferred approaches to learning

particular forms. Course designers and tutors need to enhance their capacity to deal with these individual preferences, difficult and time consuming though this may appear to be. Consider each of the headings in Figure 8.1.

Exercise

1 With which of them do you agree or disagree? Why?
2 Do your current courses meet these desirable criteria?
3 Are there any of the criteria which you now think you should apply to any or all of your courses?
4 To what extent do you perceive your courses to be integrated into a total management development philosophy, and a total management development system?

TOO PARADOXICAL FOR TRAINERS AND EDUCATORS?

It could be argued here that we are presenting a paradox. It is recommended that trainers and educators should focus on the real interests and levels of understanding of managers, rather than starting from their understanding. This appears to suggest that trainers and educators should ignore their own preferences and adapt their interests and needs to those of managers. One answer is that this approach is likely to be more effective. Another is that we should see ourselves as marketing a service, not selling what we want to produce.

Since managers' and trainers' needs and interests do differ, it would be not merely paradoxical but hypocritical if this chapter did not attempt to meet the different levels of understanding, belief or need of different kinds of trainer and educator. So the next section gives some examples of the more traditional 'skills and knowledge' route.

SKILLS-DIRECTED MANAGEMENT TRAINING

Two of the most familiar parts of an organization's management training catalogue, or consultants' or training centres' brochures, are:

- a basic course on management
- a communications skills course

Here are two examples (the second is phrased in terms of objectives rather than content):

> *Effective management 1*
> Course objectives and individual objectives
> Motivation – group discussion and research findings
> Management styles
> Decision making – alternative processes
> Team and group processes
> Setting objectives
> Individual performance review/appraisal
> Participant action plans
>
> *Communication skills 2*
> By the end of the course participants will be able to:
> - use questions to collect information from others
> - demonstrate effective listening by monitored feedback
> - be able to identify appropriate styles of chairmanship for meetings
> - be able to operate conversational control behaviour as individual member and as chairman
> - be able to make a five-minute presentation with a 70 per cent satisfaction rating from fellow participants

These are examples of courses familiar to many management trainers because they respond to the kind of needs often encountered in organizations. They can be run either in company or outside (see below for further discussion). Such programmes have considerable advantages in their own right, even though they do not meet the criteria suggested earlier. The advantages are:

- They deal explicitly with areas of skill and knowledge
- They do so within a format and a level of understanding which are relatively familiar to sponsoring managers who may have attended similar programmes themselves
- Once managers are persuaded to look at skills and knowledge needs, programmes like this provide a clear response to those defined needs
- They fit the relatively neat structure of the way of developing

skills and knowledge which many managers will understand from experience in schools and universities
- They provide relatively clear boundaries on what is to be covered, so that sponsors, participants and trainers are able to share a degree of comfort about 'how far the course will go'

The second example illustrates progress over the last twenty years; increasing attention is given to describing measurable objectives rather than just listing apparently appropriate content. Although not without problems, this has the great advantage of focusing attention on what people will be able to do, and therefore offers a basis for subsequent evaluation.

VALUES

Skills- and knowledge-centred design seems best fitted to single loop learning (see page 6); if the real need is for double loop learning (which challenges current wisdom), then the apparent benefits may be outweighed by disadvantages.

In-company courses can be particularly powerful in protecting and sustaining the culture and value system of the company. Indeed, this is precisely what some courses explicitly, but more often unconsciously, attempt to do. They are really saying 'this is a splendid organization for which to work and here are the reasons why'. They may also say, explicitly or implicitly, 'here is the way we want things done round here – do not expect to get rewarded or promoted if you behave differently'.

One of the problems for management trainers is that although courses can promote particular kinds of values, and attack others, the values concerned may not be those of the organization. Some management trainers have values which they perceive as appropriate for organizations, and seek to promote change. Thus many management trainers believe that participative management processes are better than autocratic ones, that an open style of management is better than not discussing issues, that you secure better results by kicking problems around rather than imposing solutions. These may be the values of the organization – or they may not. Even if they are the stated values they may not have much to do with the actuality of the organization.

THE LINK WITH INDIVIDUAL NEEDS

One virtue of the effectiveness-centred approach is that it is more
likely to secure the real participation of individuals on the course.
The effectiveness approach does not necessarily mean starting with
a vague session on 'Managerial effectiveness in our organization'.
Instead the programme may start with a session on 'What is our
business and what do we need to do to manage it well?' or 'What
are the problems and opportunities facing our organization and
what do we need to do well to meet them?'

While this approach may mitigate it will not overcome the
different problems so frequently encountered on many management
courses: failures in the nomination and preparation process. Management trainers and educators usually point to the nominator as the
cause of the problem. Managers arrive on courses at short notice
having been told 'it was their turn' and with no previous discussion
with their bosses about why they are being sent. Some people for
whom the course is, in fact, appropriate turn up but are poorly
motivated; and sometimes people turn up for whom the course is
not appropriate at all. When every allowance has been made for
the exigencies of managerial life, which does sometimes mean that
nominations have to be changed at the last moment, there are too
many occasions when people who could have been given adequate
notice were not. It is scarcely surprising that someone whose needs
have not been discussed is at best unlikely to see how a course may
help or at worst disposed to reject the course precisely because it
has been imposed without discussion.

THE EFFECTIVENESS APPROACH ILLUSTRATED

We return now to four examples of the effectiveness approach. The
first has been deliberately chosen to illustrate how a concern for

effectiveness, i.e. what managers actually can be helped to do, caused a change in the design of the programme. I have encountered the original design in a number of other organizations. It was in most cases clear that they had not identified the basic concept of their programme as effectiveness. They had seen this particular part of the programme as a useful culminating feature, with all the trappings of presentations to the chief executive. They also had seen it as essentially about imparting knowledge on the company strategy, which is regarded as a useful thing to do with middle or senior managers. Both these are legitimate objectives. The change illustrated in the first case study below followed from a different understanding about the usefulness of focusing on effectiveness, and a different view about the priority of doing so in comparison with 'handing knowledge out'.

Case 1

The final stages of a two-week management development programme were originally geared to the participants reviewing the corporate strategy of the group for
which they worked. The intention of the sessions, which
included a presentation to the chief executive, was that
participants should be more familiar with the thinking
behind the corporate strategy. It seemed to me less
relevant that participants should understand the corporate strategy than that they should be encouraged to take
action on strategic issues affecting their own business. So
a change was made. Participants were asked to make
proposals on a significant business problem currently
affecting most of them. One group was asked to work
on the nature of, and possible reactions to, competition
from Japanese manufacturers. While they could not do
anything to affect corporate strategy, except perhaps
understand it better, they could do something in their
own companies about the Japanese 'threat'.

Case 2

A company which had revised its sales objectives and
organization structure was concerned that the managers
involved might not have the skills necessary to achieve
the changed objectives. Analysis made it clear that,
although a number probably were lacking in some skills,
the more crucial problem was that, although apparently

committed to the revised objectives, they had not fully
set up the action plan necessary to implement them.
The prime effectiveness concern was not therefore the
skills of sales management, but the identification of
action to implement the broad objectives agreed.

Case 3

A company which had changed the composition and
structure of its marketing function found that a number
of those involved would be unable to produce what
was required because they did not have the requisite
marketing skills. In the course of discussion with them
the emphasis was shifted from the acquisition to the
implementation of skills. An in-house marketing programme was devised which, as well as giving managers
the necessary tools, helped them identify specific
marketing projects which needed to be undertaken. The
programme was designed to meet the general marketing
skill requirements of the organization, the specific
requirements of the projects which had to be undertaken
and the completion of real work to meet the needs of
the business.

Case 4

MBA programmes normally provide participants with
a better understanding of the various functional areas of
management like marketing, finance and production. It
is expected that managers who have acquired this
knowledge will be able to manage these functions
better or, through a better understanding, improve
their relationships with other departments. The MBA
programme run at International Management Centres
starts at the other end of the process by requiring our
associates to analyse the nature of relationships between
their own function and others in the business, and to
make proposals for improvement. While we believe that
it may be important for most managers to 'understand
finance better', we see it as at least as important that
they should be helped to take specific actions relevant
to their needs in dealing with other functions.

Exercise

1 What is your experience in dealing with needs similar to those described here?
2 Has the description of focusing on effectiveness, and the illustratons given here, given you different ideas for handling similar problems in the future?

EDUCATION OR TRAINING?

In the past, education has been defined as a broadly based and broadly directed process aimed at the whole person and total career, while training has been seen as the specific process of helping managers to learn things appropriate to particular circumstances, within specific organizations or industries. The distinction also broadly followed location: education was what happened in the further education system and training was what happened in management centres.

The distinction, if ever true, seems now to have largely lost its meaning. Although training centres probably tend to focus more on issues that are practical and specifically related to organizational needs, they also often see themselves as educating a manager for his or her total life. Similarly, education centres have increasingly taken on responsibility for developing managers who meet the specific needs of their particular organizations. One of the most obvious illustrations of this has been in the attitude of the major traditional business schools. When first set up they took a distinctly lofty and distant view about the desirability of doing in-company work (except as private ventures by senior faculty). Now all of them make a virtue, as well as a great deal of money, from giving such work prominence.

Until relatively recently a different distinction could have been drawn between education and training. Education processes, particularly as exhibited on MBA programmes, were clearly knowledge based, whereas training was much more likely to have a higher skill content and be more directly concerned with implementation. But under the impact of customer resistance, there has been a considerable conceptual and practical shift towards skills of implementation and effectiveness. Revans's attacks from outside the system on traditional business school processes were significant because they provided a distinctive phrase – action learning –

and a description of managerial learning processes which was intellectually as well as practically attractive. Not that Revans was successful in converting any existing business school, nor indeed that he had a major impact on other business schools for a number of years. Nor did the parallel work of John Morris (at the Manchester Business School), who showed in his *Joint development activities*[1] that the essential concepts of action learning could be incorporated into at least part of a business school. Indeed, Morris's ideas remained a special feature rather than being incorporated into the total philosophy of his business school.

It took a privately funded business school (International Management Centres) to go wholeheartedly for the action learning concept. Other business schools have on the whole tried to tack some action learning concepts and methodologies on to otherwise traditional MBA programmes. In most cases this has meant adding a project, a process which can take students into the area of reality and effectiveness.

It might be thought that I am simply engaging in special pleading for the kind of work my own institution does. We are, however, a particular illustration of the general case I am making, of the necessity for moving business schools towards reality and effectiveness. In addition to those business schools which now incorporate a project, 1988 saw the launch of a new MBA programme at City University with a dramatically different view about the appropriate composition of an MBA programme, based on a competency approach and allowing for a variety of inputs drawn from existing management training programmes.

MBA programmes receive disproportionate attention in discussion about management education and training because they are the longest and most ambitious attempt to develop managers by structured processes. Measured in terms of growth of numbers since 1966, and in terms of a substantial proportion of client reaction, traditional MBA programmes can scarcely be said to have made a major contribution in the UK. Even in the United States there are major concerns about the actual results achieved by 80,000 MBA graduates a year, and this concern has been expressed not so much by concerned industrialists as by academic researchers like Behrman and Levin.[2] The proposals in the Constable Report[3] to quintuple production of MBA graduates in the UK seems rather odd. This report lacked any analysis of why management training and education processes have so far been unattractive to British management. Without such an analysis it is difficult to see why merely multiplying the number of formal management education processes on offer would increase the number wishing to take advantage of them. What is needed is a fundamental shift towards reality and effectiveness – issues identified by organizations giving evidence to Constable, not merely the obsessive views of this particular author!

Of course, a great deal of good management education is achieved outside the major business schools. We are paying attention here to such schools and to shifts within them because those schools are inevitably in a leadership position.

It should finally be emphasized that since it is a theme of this book that individuals differ, their capacity to learn from particular kinds of programme and their interest in doing so will also differ. The traditional business school programmes, with their heavy emphasis on knowledge, rationality and analytical skills, may well be more appropriate to some individuals than courses of the kind which I have tended to argue for in this chapter.

OWN ORGANIZATION AND OPEN PROGRAMMES

This book's stress on the contingent reality of management – that what a manager needs to be able to do well in one organization may differ significantly from requirements in another – suggests that in-company programmes are more likely to meet these needs successfully. Not all organizations will in fact have a choice, because they may not be of sufficient size for it to be economical or feasible to gather all managers together for a formal training course. Where organizations are large enough, they will probably opt for a mix of in-company and outside courses. Virtues and defects are readily identifiable, as shown in Figure 8.2. The problem is to distinguish which apply to particular purposes and individuals. A good review of pros and cons is given in Hussey.[4]

Exercise

1 Consider an experience in your own development, where you can compare the benefits of own organization and open programmes. How far do these match the points made in Figure. 8.2?
2 Consider an experience of someone who you may have nominated to attend a course. To what extent were the issues covered in the figure considered, and with what result?
3 What action may you take in the future as a result of these first two questions?

Figure 8.2   Comparison of 'Own Organization' and Open Programmes

Own organization	Open
Potentially specific to organization needs	Likely to be general
Can make use of company-specific material	Use material from a variety of sources
Contained within organizational culture	May develop alternative views about organization culture
Probably focuses on company issues	Operates more widely in a general context
Participants more likely to feel they are being assessed	Participants more likely to feel they are not being assessed
Experience on offer is relatively narrow	Experience available from managers and faculty likely to be wider
Economic for groups of managers	Suitable for 'single' managers
Tutors may be perceived as 'junior'	Higher quality and/or credibility of tutors

LINE MANAGEMENT OWNERSHIP

It is preferable for nominations to arise through a well conducted appraisal or personal development review. If managers respond to the arrival of a course brochure, and suggest it either for themselves or for someone else, this relatively opportunistic process can be successful, if there is proper discussion. The worst nomination position is that of 'Buggins's turn'; there are still organizations where someone attends a course because all senior managers do and it is now his or her turn to go.

There are four other aspects of the contribution of line management:

- design of internal courses
- participation
- production of case material
- counterpart role

It is very helpful, particularly for senior programmes, to involve a senior line manager who is perceived as the programme's main client in its design. The line manager would not be expected to contribute in terms of method, but he or she should validate the content.

It is often easier to get line managers to participate in laying on the course. The formal role has tended to be that of giving a talk; but line managers are now increasingly invited as receivers of syndicate reports or reviewers of projects. Not all of them are good at this (any more than they are at giving a talk); but this latter role is much more relevant to management processes. Those for whom pressure or lack of competence make a formal role inappropriate can be invited to contribute informally, perhaps by attending dinners during the course. Individual managers can be asked to help develop particular case study material to be used on the programme. This might be gathered directly from their files or drawn out of them by discussion.

In my own organization we have developed the concept of a 'counterpart'. This is a senior line manager or director who acts as a twin with our faculty: for example the organization's marketing director works closely with our marketing tutor. We have found this a particularly helpful process in sorting out the real issues and priorities in a business; we get further reinforcement that what is done on the course accords with organizational priorities rather than those which we as experts might impose.

OPEN AND DISTANCE LEARNING

These two approaches are often coupled, although in fact they are neither the same thing nor even mutually dependent! Snell and Binsted[5] define open learning as to do with learners having:

- choice about which learning goals they pursue
- choice about sequence or depth of learning
- choice about learning processes and depth of their involvement
- unrestricted access from the educational point of view, e.g. no entry qualifications

Distance learning
- involves the geographical separation of the tutor and the learner
- involves the use of at least one form of media (print, video, computer output)
- is suitable for solo learners (although can be used in small groups of two or more)
- needs a delivery system
- works anywhere providing appropriate hardware is available

Given these definitions, it is confusing that the Open University and the Open College are so called. The titles derive from the *intention* of the offer rather than the *nature* of the process. A number of the concepts involved in the description of open learning will be addressed further in Chapter 11 in relation to self-development.

It is relevant here to offer some brief comments on distance learning. The packages which were developed from the early 1980s were initiated and publicized as a flexible and cost-effective way of dealing with large volume training requirements. Very large sums of money were spent on the development of the major packages. The programmes were intended to cope with the fact that managers do not find it convenient to attend courses, but could be stimulated by the opportunity to learn from visually presented material at home or at work. However, evaluation so far shows considerable wastage and ineffectiveness. Mann, in an article based on her original research,[6] showed that only one-third of students actually completed their study. The article spells out the reasons for failure, some of which are not peculiar to distance learning: They relate to the now familiar issues of relevance to need and the nomination process. Packages have to be general in order to sell to a general population; but inevitably they then become less useful for some participants.

There are two further important points about the learning process. The largely solitary nature of learning means that participants often lack precisely those additional inputs, challenges and supporting behaviours which they would get in a group process. As Snell and Binsted state, preferred learning styles are also a major issue. Some learners will find the solitary, reflective, non-participative, non-action-oriented process acceptable, and others will not.[7]

DESIGN ISSUES

Managers' criticism of courses has often centred on the issue of reality. Sometimes the word is seen as coterminous with relevance; but strictly speaking they are different concepts. Relevance relates to a manager's perception of whether the content or some part of the content of a course engages with issues that are important in the job. As we have argued throughout this book, this is of major importance. However, reality is something different. Content could be relevant, as described above, but still be seen as unrealistic compared with how the manager perceives things actually to work.

Team-building processes illustrate the difference. Most managers work in groups, and many work in what are intended to be teams. Team-building sessions are therefore likely to have high relevance potential. (Although actual relevance will, of course, depend on whether managers perceive team issues as being actually important in current performance.) However, the particular process used for developing ideas about, and techniques for, effective teamwork might be seen as unreal. For many years trainers have used simulation exercises whose prime purpose is to promote reflection about teamwork. The construction of the tallest tower in Lego bricks, or the longest unsupported bridge, or outdoor training are examples. All of them deal with the 'relevant' issues of teamwork, but all of them have been criticized as unreal.

Reality becomes an inherent inescapable problem when managers do anything other than 'real' work. All processes involving exercises whether of the kinds mentioned above, or role plays, case study analysis, business games, simulate, but are not managerial reality. They are an attempt to provide, in a structured learning environment, something which is believed to tackle the issues or to demonstrate the skills involved in real management work. There are at least three problems about simulations:

- They are clearly designed by and in the control of the tutor. They involve games playing, and games played to rules set by the tutors not by managers
- They are sometimes offered not primarily as a means of best meeting a specific objective, but as a means of providing variety within a longer programme, or as a rather crude means of involving managers
- As with any other learning process, individuals respond differently. Some are incapable of abstracting from unreality and drawing out useful lessons, while others accept the unreality and are able to generate useful learning experiences

Effective management training and education recognizes and attempts to deal with these problems. A thorough-going analysis is provided in the series of articles by Binsted and Stuart.[8] Huczynski's *Encyclopedia* illustrates the extraordinary variety of techniques available.[9] We should not abandon simulations, or any other process, simply because they are unreal. But any simulation technique should be used with a much more careful attention to objectives and learner preferences than seems often to be the case. Management trainers should consider first if it is possible to use reality rather than simulate it. It is a legitimate argument that the triviality of tasks such as building with Lego bricks or making paper aeroplanes is necessary so that managers do not get so obsessed with the task that they avoid the learning. There are circumstances in which that argument is a clinching one. If, however, we tried to make more frequent use of real-work experiences within a programme – and a project is an obvious example – then:

- We would be less frequently criticized by managers for designing unreal situations
- We would reduce the notorious 'transfer' problem
- We would actually enable managers to go away having achieved a real managerial task, rather than having received the award for the most effective bridge or map-reading exercise

DESIGNING LEARNING INTO COURSES

One of the problems with management training and education has been a tendency to accept generalizations about learning and an absence of serious work on the learning process, its application in the course context and its interpretation for particular individuals. It is extraordinary that we have had only one major institutional contribution to our understanding of learning, the collection of individual and research projects conducted at the Centre for the Study of Management Learning at Lancaster. Learning is apparently a subject unworthy of attention by our major business schools.

Some of the main aspects of the learning process were indicated in Chapter 2, and are developed much more fully in Chapter 11. The main points here are:

- Courses can and should be designed around explicit learning concepts, not on superficial and anecdotal statements such as 'managers like to learn by doing things'
- The recognition that managers differ in their current capacity to learn from different types of learning experience does not need to remain at the level of a crude generalization. It is unacceptably facile and lazy to throw a variety of processes into a course on the grounds that variety is a good thing and that this will ensure that no one is bored all the time
- The capacity of individuals to learn from particular processes is predictable, identifiable, observable and discussable. This capacity can be diagnosed, as Mumford describes[10]

The view that a course should consider every variety of managerial skill without attempting to discuss, let alone develop, the one common skill necessary for the development of all the others is ludicrous once stated. Yet there are still many courses where the opportunity to work on individual learning is ignored. (See, for example, nearly all traditional MBA programmes.) This is illustrated in articles about two quite different courses.

The first, by Honey and Lobley,[11] describes the intensive nature of the learning review process adopted on a redesigned outdoor management course. In view of the surge of popularity of outdoor training in the 1980s, this article is most important in showing how understanding of the learning process, and therefore learning itself, can be enhanced. A problem with all too many outdoor courses has been that the excitement over the physical activity has far overwhelmed any learning benefit. Butler's article[12] describes a different kind of management development programme, very much more in the mode of traditional three-week programmes for senior functional managers.

EVALUATION

The previously traditional separation between validation – people learning what you intend them to learn – and evaluation – has what they learned been put into useful effect? – was referred to in Chapter 7. In principle both activities are much easier in relation to a structured learning event like a course. It does, however, seem to be the case that only a tiny proportion of courses are subject to either. Easterby-Smith reviews both the reasons for evaluation and some of the reasons why it is found difficult.[13] Reasons why evaluation is rarely conducted include:

- the absence of clear objectives and standards of achievement for the course
- lack of interest by line managers, who have not forced trainers to provide clear statements of benefits achieved
- a lack of interest among trainers and educators, who are characteristically more interested in delivering the course than reviewing the results. It may be significant here that on the Honey/Mumford learning styles scores, trainers score relatively low on the reflector score, indicating a lack of interest in collecting data
- the actual difficulty in constructing relevant analytical processes

Many trainers and educators still use what are in effect 'happiness sheets'. These review participants' perceptions of the quality of tutors, the effectiveness of particular techniques used, the range of facilities provided and perhaps some summary of learning points achieved. Although not totally without merit, in that they assist decision making about the future employment of particular tutors, for instance, they do not provide either validation or evaluation. They actually provide best of all something which has nothing to do with either – an opportunity for course participants to say something and to feel that they are contributing to the future development of the course.

This is an area which remains a problem. There is every logical reason for giving more attention and more resources to it, and yet trainers and educators have survived for years without. Sensible and helpful guidance in the materials indicated is available; what is lacking is the personal motivation to undertake it.

FORMAL LEARNING WITHOUT COURSES

There are a number of learning opportunities away from work, such as those spelled out in Chapter 7. Just as individuals can, through a formal management development scheme, be placed on particular task forces or committees, so they can be appointed to outside committees. They can be encouraged to join in the work of voluntary or charitable organizations. They can be sent as representatives to industry associations. The formal system can encourage the sensible choice of people in terms of development not just in terms of their capacity to represent the organization. But just as with the analogous internal activities, these things will remain only partially used opportunities if they incorporate no process for facilitating learning.

Compared with all the other material in this chapter, the distinguishing characteristic here is that these managerial or quasi-managerial activities are not designed specifically as learning experiences. Learning is therefore less likely to occur, even if the formal system makes the individual aware of the learning opportunity, unless the steps shown in Chapter 11 are taken.

You may like to ask yourself the following questions about your organization.

Exercise

1 Have we reviewed recently our use or non-use of courses? What, in our experience, are the most powerful reasons for using courses at all, or for not using them?
2 What system do we currently use for assessing whether to have own organization or open programmes of our provision of courses?
3 For which purposes is one more suitable than the other?
4 What use do we currently make of the other learning opportunities outside work (see Figure 6.1)?

REFERENCES

1 MORRIS J. 'Joint development activities'. In BECK J. and COX R., *Advances in management education*. Wiley, 1980
2 BEHRMAN J. N. and LEVIN R. I. 'Are business schools doing their job?' *Harvard Business Review*. January–February 1984
3 CONSTABLE J. *The making of British managers*. BIM/NEDO, 1987
4 HUSSEY D. *Management training and corporate strategy*. Pergamon, 1988
5 SNELL R. and BINSTED D. *Issues in management development*. CSML, 1985
6 MANN S. 'Why open learning can be a turn off'. *Personnel Management*. January 1988
7 SNELL and BINSTED, *op cit*
8 BINSTED D. and STUART R. 'Designing reality into managerial learning events'. *Personnel Review*, Vol 8, Nos 3 and 4, 1979 and Vol 9 No 1, 1980
9 HUCZYNSKI A. *Encyclopedia of management development methods*. Gower, 1983
10 MUMFORD A. 'Learning to learn for managers'. *Journal of European Industrial Training*. Vol 10, No 2, 1986
11 HONEY P. and LOBLEY R. 'Learning from outdoor activities'. *Industrial and Commercial Training*. November 1986
12 BUTLER J. 'Learning more effectively on a general management programme'. *Industrial and Commercial Training*. July 1988
13 EASTERBY-SMITH M. *Evaluation of management education training and development*. Gower, 1986

9 People Who Help Development

The prime responsibility for ensuring that managers develop their abilities and potential to the full rests with themselves – and they know it. From the mid-1970s this recognition has been accompanied by a changed recognition of the nature and impact of formal development processes.

The early writers on managerial self-development were stimulated by different views and experiences. The processes and issues involved, and the general principles of what individuals should do for themselves, are covered in Chapter 11. It is crucial here to recognize that the role of all the people mentioned in this chapter is secondary to the role of the individual. While this may seem wholly obvious and acceptable in relation to informal and accidental development activities, it is also true of the role that others may play in encouraging, delivering and monitoring formal management development processes. This is a fact which it is easy to accept in principle, but which for a variety of reasons those involved often find difficult to implement in practice.

Exercise

1 Do you agree that primary responsibility for development rests with the individual, not with any helper?
2 How far do you think the management development processes in which you are involved actually demonstrate this?
3 Consider two experiences in which you may have been involved:
   - if you have been running a course, to what extent have individuals been encouraged to define their own needs, and identify their own solutions?
   - if you have been involved in counselling an individual's development, what has been his or her involvement in defining needs and identifying solutions?

It is likely that the response of some readers to this exercise will have been that 'of course it is a matter of balance'. So the next question is:

4 How far do you think the individuals you have identified in the exercise above would feel that they were in charge of their own development, as compared with accepting your well designed and helpful interventions?

A RANGE OF HELP AND HELPERS

In this chapter an extensive range of people who may help is reviewed, as is a number of the processes by which they may offer help. The chapter covers help offered within the formal processes, but also shows how help can be given to improve learning on the job in the Type 2 mode. Figure 9.1 shows the range of people who might be involved.

Figure 9.1 Potential Helpers in Development

On the job	Off the job
• boss	• tutors/trainers/facilitators
• grandboss	• consultants
• professional advisers – internal	• friends
• professional advisers – external	• spouse
• mentors	
• colleagues	
• subordinates	
• management development committee	

The actual roles of the people indicated in Figure 9.1 are clearly different; but it is useful to note that their type of responsibility is also different.

- *The Boss* normally has an explicit, and certainly an implicit, managerial responsibility for helping the development of subordinates. The responsibility is attributed, but in practice avoidable.
- *Professional helpers* also carry formal responsibility, which can again be explicit or implicit. Compared with the boss, however, they lack for most purposes direct power: they usually influence decisions rather than making them about the development of individuals. In most cases their responsibility is seen as entirely concerned with formal processes. This is partly because of

perceptions about the nature of management development.

- *Other helpers* are essentially volunteers. They may either offer help or respond to implied or explicit requests for help. With the exception of mentors on some occasions they are normally part of the informal and accidental processes of management development. They are a most significant part of that dominant process, but they have no formal responsibility. With the boss, they are the prime means of securing more effective development from real managerial activities.

The Boss

The example of Reg Jones, Chief Executive of General Electric, was quoted on page 92. Here was a man at the top of one of the largest companies in the world engaging in the formal process of identifying a successor for himself. He also described the managerial work he had assigned to potential successors as part of that process. This is an example of the formal responsibility of the boss, although the actual example showed only part of that responsibility. As we have seen so often throughout this book, much formal development is about providing opportunities, but not about ensuring that those opportunties are properly utilized and understood. Perhaps Reg Jones did discuss what was involved from a learning, as well as performance, point of view; but he did not say so.

Formal management development systems emphasize the role of the boss. This is correct, since a unique managerial responsibility rests with the boss. While we have fortunately long passed the days when the boss was actually seen as 'responsible' for the development of subordinates, rather than for helping their development, the system is quite right to place the boss at the forefront of formal processes.

What has predictably been less understood and provided for is what actually happens in terms of learning from real managerial work. Formal systems have allocated formal responsibility for particular kinds of development role, because it is perceived that without the allocation of such formal responsibility appropriate action will not be taken. Proper though this is, it has left as either unrecognized or untilled the rich field of learning from normal managerial work and the day-by-day relationship between boss and subordinate. The particularly powerful nature of this relationship in learning terms was frequently evidenced in my research with directors although they often harked back to their days as young or middle managers, rather than to recent experiences. An effective management development process would therefore not only encourage bosses to take up their formal managerial responsibility in the Type 3 mode, but would also encourage them to improve the contribution they make in their day-to-day informal relationships. Processes necessary for converting the boss's contribution from Type 1 to Type 2 are shown in Figure 9.2.

Figure 9.2   Roles of a Manager in Developing Subordinates

Within formal system of development (Type 3)

- appraisal of performance
- appraisal of potential
- analysis of development needs and goals
- recognizing opportunities
- facilitating those opportunities
- giving learning a priority

Within the direct managerial context (Type 2)

- using management activities as learning
- establishing learning goals
- accepting risks in subordinate performance
- monitoring learning achievement
- providing feedback on performance
- acting as a model of managerial behaviour
- acting as a model of learning behaviour
- using learning styles
- offering help
- direct coaching

One additional gloss on the distinction between Type 2 and Type 3 offered in the figure may be helpful. Formal management development processes require the manager to take on additional managerial tasks, called management development. In Type 2 processes, the boss is not taking on additional managerial activities but using existing ones.

This description of the role of the boss has so far focused entirely on direct personal contribution. Of course the collective of managers, and particularly the board of directors, has the responsibility for actually determining the nature of management development in their organization. Their responsibility for the total system, again usually seen purely in terms of the formal processes set up for the organization as a whole, is also important, though different in kind from that discussed so far. The general rather than personal involvement of the boss in the total system will include:

- helping to determine the formal management development system, and perhaps contributing to a written policy
- giving evidence of the priority attached to management development by allocating resources, participating in decision-making meetings and courses
- giving personal evidence of interest by calling for reports on what has been done and evaluating results, by discussing development issues with managers at various levels on both a formal and an informal basis, by making achieved development of subordinates one of the criteria for selection for promotion

Of course not all bosses provide all the support and encouragement which is desirable in either of the modes described in the figure.

Here is an exercise which readers can carry out for themselves and which they could also use with other managers.

Exercise

1　Consider the items in Figure 9.2 and assess yourself on a scale 0 = not done well, 10 = consistently done excellently. (This obviously assumes that you do have subordinates.)
2　Assess your own boss on the same basis.
3　What conclusions do you draw for yourselves and in relation to your boss?
In most cases what a boss provides is really a Type 1 experience. Here are two examples:
　'One of my early bosses made me swim managerially. He pushed me in, though I knew he would not let me drown.'
　'One boss taught me how to prepare a case, because nothing got past him unless every dot and comma checked out. Another boss later taught me that you could ask for a clear case yet show trust in the guy who was delivering it instead of distrust.'
4　What conclusions do you draw from these two cases about the kind of development being offered to the subordinates?
5　What advice might you give the boss in each case in order to improve the learning experience?
6　What advice would you give subordinates to increase their achieved learning from this relationship?

As these last two cases also show, the boss/subordinate relationship, as far as achieved development is concerned, is most likely to centre around achieved performance because that is how managers assess themselves and others. It is precisely because performance is so fundamental to the relationship that it is potentially the crux of the learning relationship; it is, however, also the cause of difficulty in the learning process because performance so often outweighs the learning issues involved.

You might like to try the following exercise on a manager's responsibility for developing subordinates.

Exercise

Jack Simpson went into the Chief Executive's office expecting promotion. He was in charge of the largest product group in his division. His career had been one of rapid advancement, through a series of successes, usually in jobs which he held for about eighteen months.

His contributions to the success of the areas in which he worked were shown by the fact that his results were usually better than his predecessors' and performance often slipped back after he had left a job.

The potential new job had many of the characteristics of those in which he had succeeded previously. At each stage of his career he had shown that he could handle bigger and tougher jobs.

1   Is there any evidence in the information given here to suggest he should not be promoted?
2   What recommendations would you make about Jack Simpson?
3   What evidence is there about either his own development or that of other people?

The Grandboss

In the formal management development system, the boss's boss has the managerial responsibility for checking that his subordinate manager is developing his subordinates. The formal system normally requires that appraisal forms are reviewed and, if necessary, amended by the grandboss (a title I have chosen in preference to grandfather or grandmother). Of course the grandboss is expected to do more than chase, by providing personally a good example of attention to Type 3 processes.

The grandboss may often exercise a balancing role, giving, for instance, a longer-term view about the desirability of a particular job or assignment for someone further down the line. The grandboss can sometimes have different priorities about the desirability of a manager attending a course at a difficult time, or being placed on a committee or working party when she or he is not the most obvious nomination but would benefit in development terms. Finally, of course, the grandboss can help improve learning on the job by demonstrating the relevant managerial and learning abilities and by asking the right question in the course of normal managerial activity.

Internal Professional Advisers

Personnel specialists, management development advisers, management trainers and human resources specialists of a variety of titles are covered in this section. The personnel director ought to direct the development processes and ensure that any separate specialisms are coordinated. This responsibility is not always met, especially where training and development are compartmentalized. The different roles depend on the size of the organization and more particularly on the amount of resources it is prepared to put into this whole field.

I do not provide a detailed summary of the activities of a management development adviser in this chapter. This may seem a surprising omission. I believe that to do so would duplicate the suggestions offered and the exericises included throughout the book. The following comments therefore build on issues covered earlier.

An organization which takes formal development seriously will seek advice from internal professionals on:

- the objectives, philosophy and nature of desired management development in the organization
- the formal schemes, policies and procedures necessary to support those objectives
- the resources necessary to put formal processes into effect – internal staffing, selection and use of consultants, the strategy for internal as opposed to external courses
- the quality of resources provided: 'which is the best course for senior executives?', 'which consultant has the best reputation for dealing with these particular issues?'
- establishing benefits and evaluating results

In some cases internal professionals will act as counsellors or advisers to managers on problems concerned with effective performance. So a management development adviser might help set up a two-day event 'Problems and opportunities to 1995', or 'Clarifying relationships between our divisions'. The adviser might give individual advice on development, in terms of a total career plan or in terms of advice on a particular need or a developmental process.

The internal adviser can only successfully help those interested in receiving help. Unfortunately the status of some internal advisers constrains their effectiveness. Their status often reflects the organization's view about their capacity to help at more senior levels – a view which may be changed if the adviser offers help on issues of real concern. It is surprising to find that there is little literature on what management development advisers do, as compared with a significant amount on trainers.

There are two additional areas of knowledge which the adviser really ought to have. The first is *a knowledge of not only the principles, but the working practices of management*. The credibility of advisers is nearly always assisted if they have actually worked in something other than management development or personnel. The qualification 'nearly always' allows for those unfortunate circumstances where the adviser is seen as a failed manager rather than an experienced manager. Whatever their background, advisers ought to have a knowledge of what actually happens in management. This is readily available in two forms: the books by Rosemary Stewart, Henry Mintzberg and John Kotter referred to in Chapter 2, or the convenient summary in Mumford.[1] The second way of acquiring knowledge is actually to get out among managers, to talk to them, to sit in on their meetings, to go on visits with them. In my experience requests of this kind are very generously welcomed; managers are flattered that you should be interested in how they actually work. It is important that you establish some rules of the game, most particularly stressing that there will be no formal or informal feedback to others in the organization.

The second area relates to *understanding learning and development processes*. The adviser should clearly be in the position of being able to recommend appropriate development solutions to whatever development needs arise, and appropriateness depends on an understanding not only of general learning principles, but of the specifics of how individuals will react. This subject is covered in more depth in Chapter 11 and in the associated further reading. One of the clear roles for the internal adviser is to show why planned development is necessary and how it has the potential to bring identifiable benefits. Some aspects of this have already been covered in Chapter 6 where we dealt with the process of analysing needs. Where these clearly show that some formal process is necessary in order to equip managers to meet the needs of the business, then a major benefit has already been established. However this is not an answer in all situations, since the connections may not be sufficiently clear and dramatic to convince senior managers. In such cases the adviser will have to fall back on some more or less sophisticated version of 'others do more':

- competitors
- my previous company
- other countries
- excellent companies

There has been a spate of reports touching on these aspects in the 1980s, starting with *A challenge to complacency*[2] and going through the Mangham Report on management training[3] and the Constable and Handy Reports.[4] It is, however, unlikely that these grand national comparisons will prod many individual organizations into action. They are more likely to respond to the examples offered in *In search of excellence*,[5] and more specifically to the development processes described by John Kotter.[6]

External Professional Advisers

One of the reasons for going outside the organization for help was indicated towards the end of the previous section. The greater the level of intimacy of the development counselling and advice, the greater the likely worry of managers about the terms under which it is offered. While the internal adviser potentially has the great advantage of knowing much more about the reality of the organization, the problem of confidentiality inevitably arises. Can a manager really get highly personal advice from an internal adviser and trust that details of his thoughts and problems are not going to be passed on or used internally? There are more positive reasons than this for going outside. The organization may simply lack internal people with the credibility or professional competence to provide the necessary advice. Or it may wish to test its internal knowledge against the wider view. Examples might be the review of an existing appraisal scheme or the introduction of a new one, an audit of existing management development practices (see Chapter 1 for an example of what might be covered) or the analysis of particular management problems, such as how a management team is actually operating. Advice on selecting and using outside resources of this kind are given in Kakabadse.[7]

Mentors

The process of mentoring was described in the previous chapter. There is now some doubt that the widespread utilization of mentors identified particularly in the American literature and followed up by the book by Clutterbuck[8] is in fact turning out to be as significant as was thought. Part of the problem is a confusion of roles: the American literature has often accorded a boss the role of mentor. Clutterbuck gives an excellent list of ideal characteristics:

- already has a good record for developing other people
- has a genuine interest in seeing younger people advance and can relate to their problems
- has a wide range of current skills to pass on
- has a good understanding of the organization, how it works and where it is going
- combines patience with good interpersonal skills and an ability to work in an unstructured programme
- has sufficient time to devote to the relationship
- can command a protégé's respect
- has his own network of contacts and influence

I would add to that list:

- has credibility as a manager
- has an understanding of the different learning processes available and the differing learning preferences of individuals

The American evidence about mentoring is discussed at greater length in the further reading. It is interesting that in both my own research[9] and that of McCall *et al.*[10] very few executives identified a mentor contribution. In the UK there has certainly not been sufficient time to test mentoring as a formal process. If it has existed it has been essentially as an informal relationship between a senior manager and a more junior other, perhaps not always even recognized as such by either party. 'I just like giving younger people a hand.'

Colleagues

Colleagues can give help when they are more experienced or more skilled in direct coaching and counselling. They may not offer such help but may well respond to a request. In most cases the help offered is not formal. It is something which arises from normal managerial activities: shared problem solving, discussion of a difficult forthcoming meeting, a chat about a difficult colleague, a review of organizational necessities and political requirements. So far as the managers are concerned it is really all about how to manage effectively – it is only afterwards that they recognize that they have learned something from a colleague in the course of such discussions.

Another form of learning from colleagues is that of modelling or observation. This can be either positive or negative: a manager may base his future behaviour on what he admires in a successful colleague, or he may base his behaviour on the opposite of an unsuccessful process. It may seem obvious, but it is important to point out that managers can pick up useful behaviour even from people they do not like and/or admire. I recall a case where the manager thought that one of his colleagues was superb at asking questions which clarified problems and issues. 'Unfortunately, when he has finished doing that he cannot seem to come to a decision. I improve my own decisions a lot by watching him at work, but not by his actual decision making.'

Perhaps the most powerful aspect of a learning relationship with colleagues revolves around the kind of feedback one offers another. Managers often have quite incorrect ideas about how they achieve what they do. Accurate feedback, particularly if presented in a helpful rather than a negative way, is the first stage of learning and a necessary precursor to learning to do things better.

Subordinates

It is understandable that managers are much more likely to quote learning from bosses and from colleagues than they are from subordinates. Again this is partly a matter of vocabulary. When a manager moves into a new job there is always a great deal of knowledge to pick up. This may be about the nature of the particular organization, internal politics, how people in the organization, particularly the new boss, behave and expect you to behave. Managers often pick these facts up from subordinates, but do not call this learning. It is more rare for them to actually pick up skills. In my own research I found just one or two directors who identified significant learning from subordinates. In one case it was in relation to a quite new function which the director had taken on. In a sense his subordinate taught him the details of what was involved. In another case a director actually learned a quite different approach to decision making – a much more surprising event.

Learning from and through others is the result of the interaction of four different elements:

- *the person's* needs and preferred ways of learning
- *particular processes* of learning on the job
- *the people involved*
- *the total learning process* – the learning cycle

Figure 9.3 Interaction in Learning

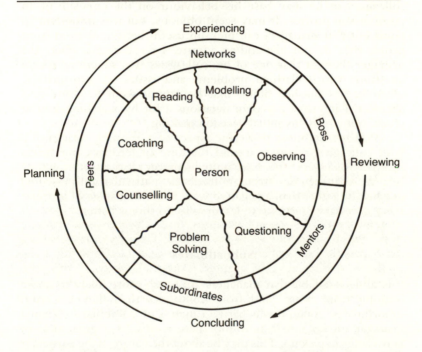

This interaction is shown in Figure 9.3. 'Networks' include the people described above as grandboss and internal and external advisers.

The traditional model of management development, with its emphasis on purely formal processes, provides a much more limited picture of the people who can help on the job and the ways in which they can help. Those management development advisers who are convinced by the alternative model of management development offered in this book will want to incorporate into their own offerings the initiation and encouragement of Type 2 processes.

COLLECTIVE INVOLVEMENT AND ADVICE

In Chapter 5, when we reviewed the elements and processes of formal management development, we referred to the probable existence of a management development committee. The point of such a committee is to:

- generate interest amongst senior management about management development
- give symbolic significance to management development
- act as the focus for decision making
- provide an opportunity to generate a consensus decision or corporate view

The kind of information presented to such committees – the use of data about individuals, summaries of appraisals, information generated from an assessment centre – has been covered in earlier chapters. Such committees are usually wholly concerned with the organization of formal opportunties, through succession planning, job rotation and nominations for courses. They are much less likely to discuss the kind of help that might be available from individuals indicated earlier in this chapter. Although such a committee therefore fills a very necessary place in the formal structure, most are stuck at the stage of defining opportunities. They do not enable managers to take advantage of those opportunities to achieve learning.

FINDING HELP OFF THE JOB

There are four types of helper away from work:

- tutors/teachers/trainers
- consultants

- friends
- spouse

Tutors, teachers and trainers have the clear formal responsibility for aiding development. The extent to which they do help development depends on:

- the needs, interests and preferred learning style of the manager being developed
- the extent to which the tutor's style and abilities relate to those needs
- the extent to which content and the process being delivered by the tutor are appropriate to the individual's needs
- the values held by the tutor, and how those values relate to the values of the manager under development

The extent to which individual tutors, or particular training centres, colleges or business schools manage to provide development appropriate to these criteria has received little attention in research. We have the painstaking and innovative work done by the Centre for the Study of Management Learning at Lancaster, exemplified by the articles by Binsted and Snell.[11] It is sad that the articles by Margerison and Lewis[12] and Hofstede,[13] which illustrate the substantially different values held by management educators as compared with their clients, have not been followed up by more detailed research. Although not based on research, Ashton's article[14] gives a persuasive review of the values held by teachers in business schools. Like Hofstede, his primary point is that the values held by business school teachers and supported by their institutions relate neither to the needs of managers in general nor to those of individual managers. It seems likely that the debate on the number of management teachers required, generated by the Handy and Constable Reports, is at least partly misplaced. As with management education itself, we should be concerned with the quality of what is being offered rather than the quantity.

As you move away from the university-centred business schools, with their strong, traditional academic values, to colleges and independent training centres, it might be claimed that because these are less academically centred they are less likely to be drawn into overly academic processes. While this may be true, it may equally be true that no other clearly identified values have replaced the academic outlook.

It may indeed be a problem for *all* institutions that their value systems are implicit rather than explicit. Perhaps because we were a new institution explicitly confronting some of the traditional beliefs about management education, my own institution has published its philosophy of management development and prints this on our conspectus.

VALUES AND BEHAVIOURS OF TUTORS, TEACHERS, TRAINERS

Exercise

1 Does your institution have a published formal statement of its philosophy of management education and training?
2 What do you perceive to be the values explicitly held by your institution, or implicit in its reward system?
3 Do you perceive there to be an actual or potential conflict between meeting immediately performance related managerial needs, as compared with broader development for the individual?
4 By what process of analysing needs has your institution established the programmes it runs?
5 Does your organization insist on formal training for its tutors?
6 What learning theory, or what beliefs about learning, apply in your institution? When were these last discussed, and where are they set out?
7 If you put the last question to your colleagues, do you believe they would answer it in terms of learning, or in terms of teaching?

Consultants

External consultants can offer help in a range of ways. They can run courses, in which case the comments made in the preceding section apply. Their other roles include:

- carrying out a management development audit, surveying the practices and policies of an organization
- carrying out an analysis of management development or training needs
- acting as a personal counsellor or mentor to individuals or to a group of managers

The objectivity, and perhaps the heightened professionalism, of the external consultants are reasons for bringing them in. The issues are similar to those discussed for tutorial roles. The actual values of the external consultant – why he or she is carrying out the role – may actually differ from the organizational requirements. For example, some consultants believe in the desirability of openness and confrontation; you may indeed seek to challenge some existing organizational norms. If this is an explicit and clear part of the contract between you, well and good. If, however, the consultant's style is not related to a clear request from you of this kind, then problems will occur. These can be avoided by open discussion and by the internal selector doing a sensible job in asking for and following up references from people for whom the consultant has carried out similar work. Casey[15] is very helpful on these issues.

Spouse

Some senior executive programmes now contain days on which the spouses of participants come for a mini-version of the programme. This kind of involvement is obviously something that affects only a tiny proportion of spouses. Much more frequently, the partner is involved in informal processes of discussion at home. There has in past decades been a considerable change in the way partners discuss careers and career moves. The advent of dual-career families is one obvious cause; but in general the trend has been towards a less clear cut, less autocratic process of decision making on the managerial career of one partner (usually male).

Most partners carry out a range of roles as listener, prompter, commentator. While some managers want to leave their work at the office and not discuss it at home, others find it at least therapeutic and sometimes positively helpful to do so. This is another largely unstudied area, and there seems to be little available other than Mumford.[16]

Friends

Friends outside work sometimes carry out the role of the mentor. Like the partner in a marriage they can provide helpful guidance on questions about career or about particular problems. Just as managers often look for someone at work who can act as a sounding board, so they may look for someone outside who carries out a similar function. Because of increasing loneliness as you move up the managerial hierarchy, the availability of such a person can be very important. This is not an aspect which has been considered in formal management development schemes, but it is one which we perhaps ought to take more seriously. We ought to provide more advice on how to identify and use potentially helpful friends, who can give advice unsullied by direct managerial responsibility (the boss) or competitiveness (colleagues). The identification of a friendly ear – my term for this relationship – could make a major future contribution to the development of managers. Many managers do use friends in this way, but informally and accidentally, perhaps as a result of a meeting on a course. Useful though those accidental processes are, they could be improved. I am not suggesting a further column in a formal management development scheme, but rather that individuals should be encouraged to think in terms of how someone outside the organization might help them identify or meet development needs. Or for those people for whom this would be too analytical and formal a process in itself, it might be enough to suggest that simple identification of a friendly ear is sufficient.

THE PROCESS OF HELPING

We need to revisit constantly the question of what a manager needs or wants (and to recognize the difference between needs and wants). We need to question what we are trying to provide and why, not only at the level of objective analysis of needs for those we are trying to help, but in terms of understanding our own purposes and motivations. Reg Revans's view of the place of consultants, lecturers or trainers in 'helping' is encompassed in his description of 'the inveterate hankering of the teacher to be the centre of attention'. (As with some other aspects of Revans's work and life there is the profound irony here, in that he is actually a superb performer as a lecturer.) This is a central point: does the offerer's help really help?

As the earlier discussion in this chapter showed, there is much too little available about the beliefs of those who are offering help. There is the article by Casey,[17] and two important contributions, particularly for the management trainer, by Honey[18] and Nixon.[19] Another expression of values can be seen in the response of trainers to the Honey and Mumford learning styles questionnaire. The norm is for trainers to be Activists (only sales managers score more highly on this dimension). Discussion on the implications of this for what trainers are offering to their clients is a powerful way of showing the values that they are probably putting over. It is even more valuable for the individual trainer to review his or her own style. (See Chapter 11 for more detailed discussion of learning styles.)

A detailed review of the actual processes through which help is offered is given in Chapter 11, since it fits more appropriately into a general review of how managers learn.

Exercise

Developing Senior Managers

You have been appointed as the first Group Personnel Director for a group of companies operating worldwide but based in London. The group has a very small corporate staff and a small main board. The executive directors comprise chairman, chief executive, finance director and four directors responsible for the main product areas of the group.

The group has had a strongly decentralized culture for fifteen years. It has a substantial record of profitable organic growth and a mixed, but largely successful, record of acquisition. Apart from yourself, all the main board directors have more than ten years' service in the group. Most, but not all, members of the main board have agreed on the need for the appointment of a personnel director. They have accepted the case for a better organized process of remuneration for the top hundred managers in the business (which employs 20,000 people worldwide). They have also decided they wanted in-house help on top level recruitment instead of relying purely on headhunters. Finally, several of them have been concerned about the development of successors to themselves and the development of people capable of taking more responsibility as the group grows.

The chairman has told you privately that he believes that a successor to the current chief executive needs to be identified and developed in the next two or three years. He hopes that the current chief executive will retire at 60 if a successor is available, although the incumbent believes he will retire at 63.

The group has for many years had a successful history of managing its growth by promotion from within, with some additional resourcing from successful acquisitions. In the last eighteen months, however, it has proved increasingly difficult to fill senior vacancies. Only a small number of names seem to be available for each appointment. As a result the group has had to go outside to recruit six managers from profit-centre companies with turnovers ranging from £25 million to £60 million.

You have spent your first month in the group visiting senior managers in many different locations around the world. You have had individual discussions with your colleagues on the board both about the priorities for your activities as they see them, and their views about what has happened so far. All of them agree that there needs to be a major push on the development of senior managers. Most of them believe that the potential is there but that it needs to be developed in some way. All of them agree that proposals for management development should be your top priority – and first submission to a forthcoming meeting of the executive directors.

Discussion with your colleagues has established that appointments to senior management positions are made by each director, subject only to agreement with the chief executive. There is no formal planning process to review top management appointments. The group has a policy of encouraging an appraisal process based on management by objectives. The chief executive does not carry this out with the other directors, but some of them follow this with their own staff. The chief executive and two of the product group directors attended the senior management programme at Henley some years previously. You have encountered one major profit centre manager who has attended the Harvard Advanced Management Programme, and he has presented to you a proposal for extensive use of business school programmes at senior level. There is no process for identifying which people should attend such programmes, nor is there so far a clear view on the utility of any such programme, except that the three main board directors value their Henley experience.

You have had a further discussion with the chairman, during which he has repeated that his main concern is to identify and develop a successor for the chief executive. He has, however, thrown in a new topic; he has asked you to look at the possibility of developing a cadre of MBAs among the middle managers in the group. He has suggested that you visit a number of business schools and select the one offering the most suitable approach.

1   How do you propose to deal with the open and hidden agendas described here?
2   What priorities would you follow and for what reasons?
3   What kind of systems and processes for management development would you recommend?
4   What arguments would you deploy for the expense and time involved in senior development?
5   Would you recruit a management development specialist to help you, or call in help from a business school or a consultant?

(This exercise is an amended version of one originally published in Personnel Management; *the author is grateful for permission to reprint it here.)*

REFERENCES

1   MUMFORD A. *Developing top managers*. Gower, 1988
2   COOPERS AND LYBRAND ASSOCIATES. *A challenge to complacency: changing attitudes to training*. A report to the Manpower Services Commission and the National Economic Development Office. MSC, 1985
3   MANGHAM I. *Management training*. University of Bath, 1986
4   HANDY C. *The making of managers*. NEDO, 1987 and CONSTABLE J. *The making of British managers*. BIM/NEDO, 1987
5   PETERS T. and WATERMAN R. *In search of excellence*. Harper and Row, 1982
6   KOTTER J. P. *The leadership factor*. Free Press, 1988
7   KAKABADSE A. 'How to use consultants'. *International Journal of Manpower*. Vol 4, No 1, 1983
8   CLUTTERBUCK D. *'Everyone needs a mentor*. 2nd ed. Institute of Personnel Management, 1991
9   Mumford, *op cit*.
10 McCALL M., LOMBARDO M. and MORRISON A. *The Lessons of Experience*. Lexington, 1988
11 BINSTED D. and SNELL R. 'The tutor learner interaction'. *Personnel Review*. Vol 10, No 3, 1981 and Vol 11, Nos 1, 2, 4, 1982
12 MARGERISON C and LEWIS R. 'Management educators and their clients'. In Beck J. and Cox R., *Advances in management education*. Wiley, 1981
13 HOFSTEDE G. 'Businessmen and business school faculty'. *Journal of Manpower Studies*. Vol 15, No 1, 1978
14 ASHTON D. 'Are the business schools good learning institutions?'. *Personnel Review*. Vol 17, No 4, 1988
15 CASEY D. 'Some processes at the consultant/client interface'. *Leadership and Organisation Development Journal*. Vol 3, No 1, 1982
16 MUMFORD A. 'Learning at home'. *Programmed Learning and Educational Technology*. Vol 22, No 4, 1985
17 *op cit*, Casey
18 HONEY P. 'What I believe about management training'. *Industrial and Commercial Training*. April 1982
19 NIXON B. 'In search of excellent management development'. *Industrial and Commercial Training*. July 1984

10 Special Needs, Different Solutions

WOMEN MANAGERS — A NATURAL DISPROPORTION?

At least 40 per cent of the UK workforce are women, according to the 1987 *Labour Force Survey*, yet at 27 per cent the proportion of women managers is much lower (and the figure of 8 per cent for women directors illustrates the point even more dramatically). There can, broadly, be two views about this disparity. One would be that the disproportionately fewer women managers and directors reflect women's actual competence or their own 'natural' career choices. A second view is that this disproportion is inappropriate either ethically or in terms of effective use of resources.

Attention to this subject is a relatively new phenomenon. Tom Roberts's book,[1] in many ways an excellent guide to orthodox management development, does not mention women at all, even in the 1974 edition. I remember the disbelief of many readers when a survey of which I was the lead author[2] suggested that the training needs of women managers might be different from those of their male colleagues. We have moved on a long way since then in terms of recognizing the issue, and to some extent in terms of understanding; but we have perhaps moved less far towards effective action. One of the problems is recognizing precisely what the issues actually are, and then what objectives might be appropriate for the development of women managers.

I can already sense the objections forming in the minds of two different types of reader. One group may be feeling that there is a simple explanation for the lower proportion of women managers, and that a more detailed analysis of the issue is unnecessary. Others may feel that to give a special section to women managers is to place them in a ghetto. In this group will be the 'cream rises to the top' sub-group, which will include some successful women. Such people tend to argue that although there are special problems for women leaders, it is the successful overcoming of those problems which demonstrates that you are special as a leader and not as a woman. They therefore deprecate any special measures to redress the balance on the grounds that they lead to tokenism or to reducing the value accorded to achieved success.

The proposition that the lower proportion of women managers is in some sense 'natural' appears in its most respectable form in terms of career choice. It is argued that women as child bearers actually leave employment at a crucial time in terms of their possible development as managers, and that many of them neither want nor expect managerial careers. Organizational attitudes which mirror that expectation are therefore thought to be understandable and proper. This view is deeply engrained in some women and in many male-dominated organizations.

However, the major shift in women's views about their own lives, and the change in their expectations and wants about their careers, have created a considerable 'push' for a change of attitude. This has been matched by 'pull' in some organizations, notably by some of the major banks. To some extent encouraged by national debate, if not action, generated by the Equal Opportunities Commission, and to some extent fuelled by recognition of their own needs, organizations are gradually becoming less accepting of traditional views about women's careers. The word 'expectations' is extremely important here. A small minority of people who are prepared to fight hard and push has gradually been augmented by a larger number whose previous negative expectations have to some extent been changed by the apparent success of the pushers.

Formal management development action taken to change both the actuality and the expectations about career opportunities for women includes:

- developing a clear policy statement directed at increasing the number of women managers and accompanying it with procedures and monitoring processes
- reviewing selection processes and selection criteria in order to control, if not eliminate, bias against women
- developing special arrangements such as extended maternity leave, career breaks with accompanying fast track training processes to enable women to return to work more quickly or more effectively

The second type of 'it is only natural' response to the lower number of women managers is more difficult to define and counter. It essentially revolves around questions of how women perform as managers and how their performance is perceived by their surrounding male colleagues. This already difficult issue is then complicated by a second question. Should women managers behave like men managers anyway, or should they behave differently? Or should more male managers try to employ the supposedly characteristic female processes evidenced by some successful women managers?

Both men and women tend to agree that women managers behave differently from their male colleagues. While women who accept the 'difference' argument will tend to say 'different but as good as', men will, more characteristically, say 'different and less effective than'. Some women managers, of course, do not accept that there is a different in how they carry out their work, and an American article[3] based on a matched study of 2,000 managers showed that women do not manage differently from men. This research evidence might seem to support the views of those successful women who tend to argue that there is no basis for claiming that women managers are different (although it says nothing about the proposition that they are actually held back).

We are faced with a number of stereotypes: of men about women, of women about men, of women about themselves. Some men point to the success of a small number of political leaders. There is, indeed, a small group of highly successful women politicians, some of them coming from even more unlikely environments than our own Margaret Thatcher. The success of Golda Meir, Indira Ghandi, Mrs Bandaraneike, Benazir Bhutto and some lesser known Scandinavian politicians may seem to support the stereotype 'it shows what can be done without laws on equal opportunities'. Yet senior women remain a tiny minority in politics, in the judiciary, in the civil service and local government.

No woman in industry or commerce has run a huge organiz-ation and received a damehood. Such female role models as there are in industry and commerce, like Anita Roddick of Body Shop or Steve Shirley of F International, tend to be important but atypical. As Marshall[4] points out, much of early discussion of women managers concentrated on the belief that men and women managers operated in essentially the same way in order to facilitate a more positive view of women's potential. She argues that these similarities have been overstated at the expense of legitimate and useful differences.

> Women tend to emphasise people management over task structuring, whilst men have opposite priorities; women are often inhibited in exercising position power because other people reject or undermine their use of authority, stereotype them in devalued female roles.

Like other authors, she comments on the male emphasis on individualism, competition and control (in contrast to interdependence, collaboration and acceptance) as defining the values to which women managers are supposed to adhere if they wish to join the managerial club.

Writers who have highlighted these competing styles and values between men and women have not made the task of management development any easier; but they may have made it more effective. They have also helped to persuade some men to view some of their own values differently. If women have the capacity not only to be different but to be usefully and effectively different by bringing to the party some female styles and values as well as some effective male attributes, might not the reverse also apply? The article by Simmons[5] shows what can be achieved by causing men to question whether breaking gender bounds will lead to more effective management.

There has been a shift among organizations and women themselves about careers and managerial jobs. There has also been an accompanying shift in the expectations of a minority of men about the women with whom they share their lives. Women will no longer necessarily surrender their careers either to the demands of child bearing or to their husbands' careers. The issue of dual-career families is the sharpest instance of this. This is particularly significant because the social circumstances of women – when they are married and have children – often make planned career development more difficult. It is understandable, although not appropriate, that the (often male) management development adviser should accept these difficulties rather than try to overcome them. Yet they are difficulties which will increasingly need to be overcome for men as well. Cavalier assumptions that men will go where they are sent, and that wives will go with them, have ceased to be tenable – for men or women.

Up till now women managers have coped with the difficulties involved in a different way from men. According to one UK survey,[6] 39 per cent of women managers were unmarried, divorced or widowed, as against 8 per cent of men (the difference is slightly larger in the United States). The appropriate inference is not that more men ought to be similarly lonely or 'available', but that this should not be an apparently necessary requirement for so many women.

The personnel function and the management development specialism point to another special feature of women managers. There has been a tendency to push them into 'caring functions'. To some extent this process is a reflection of societal stereotypes of desired female behaviour, of the failure to provide effective choice at school and of subsequent early career choice. The fact that we are more likely to find a female personnel director than production director is much more likely to be the product of these earlier factors than later career development in any particular organization. Although in some respects the role model offered by Margaret Thatcher as the toughest man in her cabinet is unfortunate, her success in carrying out her chief executive role is important. What is needed is some more role models of women moving not through the caring departments (as they used to be considered) of Education or Social Services, but through the Department of Trade and Industry, the Foreign Office and the Treasury.

WOMEN MANAGERS – DIFFERENT DEVELOPMENT NEEDS?

Women managers actually face a different situation from men managers. The predominant managerial style is most likely to be male in orientation. The women manager is therefore faced with the issue of whether, and how, to adopt managerial forms of behaviour which may contradict or conflict with her existing style of behaviour. Some women have obviously long since adopted male forms of behaviour and have no problems of such adaptation. For others the need to adapt may include:

- coping with competition
- adopting at least some of the behaviour of male clubs (post-work socializing, discussion of predominantly male sports)
- the use of personal and role power
- developing individual self-awareness
- acquiring a positive self-image as a woman manager
  — self-confidence and assertiveness skills
  — dealing with stress

The real issue for most women managers is how to handle the fact of being a woman within what is likely to be a majority group of male managers in an organization which has little sympathy for and understanding of the contribution that women might make, let alone their potentially different contribution. It should also be emphasized that at least some women managers will choose to follow the line indicated by Marshall[4] in which adaptation to male domination is not seen as the only recourse.

WOMEN MANAGERS – DIFFERENT DEVELOPMENT PROCESSES?

It is not surprising that male attitudes and behaviour on courses tend to follow the stereotypes about women found in the real world outside. Behaviour which is seen in men by men as normal, managerial assertiveness is seen by men in women as aggressive and strident. Women who do not behave according to the other kinds of stereotype are similarly pushed towards the supposedly 'feminine' behaviour corner. Women are expected to be concerned about the comfort of the group, to pour out the tea, to express emotion rather than to conceal it. They are treated with a form of superficial gallantry which emphasizes that they are being treated as a woman not as a manager. Alternatively their capacities are belittled by reference to their sexuality: 'I bet it's difficult having a serious discussion with a beauty like Jane in the group'.

Because of the difficulties women have in largely male manager-ial training and education situations, and because of the view that they have special needs anyway, women-only training groups were developed. There are two conflicting arguments over this. One says that since women have to survive in a predominantly male environment, it is unreal to provide them with women-only management training. Whatever else this may achieve, the absence of men will create a future problem of transferring any learning achieved. The alternative view is that the absence of men removes some unnecessary obstacles to learning, opens opportunities for more women to be more experimental with behaviour which may be helpful to them subsequently in the male environment. I am not aware of any research which provides a clear basis for deciding which of these views is true. There is evidence that a number of women feel they have benefited from women-only courses, in the ways indicated above. It is also the case that since some women nowadays are less prepared to accept inappropriate male behaviour towards them on courses, mixed courses can sometimes become a battleground for male/female issues rather than a learning experience related to the original objectives. It is argued on the other hand, by both men and women, that emphasizing differences by setting up women-only experiences is unhelpful.

It may be that the most useful process is to create special learning experiences for women to help them define and deal with the male world. So strategies for working cooperatively together, for understanding their relationships with men, and perhaps creating processes for challenging stereotypes all provide an appropriate focus. It is not so clear that women-only courses dealing with general management skills and requirements are desirable. Perhaps here the argument of enabling women to behave differently is less clearly dominant, as compared with the requirement for them to work even in a training context with male colleagues.

It will be noted that I am writing as a man who cannot possibly have the same recognition of the balance of feeling and requirement that a woman adviser might have. So an additional point might well be that the choice of whether to make an activity women-only should depend not only on the adviser (whether male or female) but on whether the prospective female participants actually want it that way. The case for women-only groups is well set out by Marshall.

The presence of men may be an inhibitor both to achieved learning and the expression of it by women. A related issue concerns whether women's learning processes differ from those of men. The common stereotype of the emotional and intuitive woman can be expressed in learning terms by saying that women are less responsive to hard rational approaches to learning and more responsive to particular situations and feelings. The view of women as intuitive certainly implies that their learning processes will be different from men's. One part of the answer may rest in those characteristics which women are said to share – the preference for a supportive, cooperative environment in which to learn as compared with the more characteristically competitive environment favoured by men.

However, this environmental point does not deal with the basic issue of whether women as a whole differ from men in their learning processes. On the Honey/Mumford Learning Styles Questionnaire (LSQ), the norms for 174 women differed scarcely at all from men on the Reflector and Theorist dimensions, and by only one point on the Activist (higher for women) and Pragmatist (lower for women) scores. These differences are not at a level of significance which suggests that women characteristically learn differently from men. The admittedly small sample of women in my director research similarly did not differ from their male director counterparts. The information on our LSQ is, however, different from that found by David Kolb in his Learning Styles Inventory (LSI).[7] On his dimensions, women have a much higher preference for what he calls 'abstract conceptualization', as compared with 'concrete experience'. The male scores are almost exactly opposite to the female on these dimensions. The difference in results from the LSQ may be related to the fact that the LSI brings in 'feelings' in a more overt way. My conclusion is that learning experiences should not be designed according to a stereotyped view that women will learn differently; they should be designed according to the nature of the particular group or the particular individual.

Nor is there any evidence that women learn better or worse from any particular kind of learning opportunity as compared with men. They are just as likely to learn or not learn from real tasks, projects, bosses, courses, as men are. The only area in which there may be some significant difference is that of the use of boss, colleagues or mentors. Here learning opportunities may be influenced by the stereotypes and actualities of male/female behaviour. In the scarce literature on learning from boss and colleagues there is no reference to women learning differently from men nor is it my experience that this is so. But there may well be extra inhibitions and difficulties. The only area in which this has been researched has been that of mentors. For some time it was thought that women could only get on in an organization dominated by men by having a mentor; inevitably the mentor was most often a man. More recently, of course, female mentors have become available. Again the evidence slowly coming to hand conflicts with stereotypes. The assumption that a male mentor and a female protégé will inevitably provoke jealousy in others, and particularly the suspicion that the relationship has a sexual base, has been examined by Bowey.[8] This article shows that, comparing male and female mentors of females:

- the sexual issue was not large and was quite manageable
- resentment is created irrespective of whether the mentor was male or female
- there are positive benefits for both male and female mentors and their protégés both at and outside work

Kram[9] offers rather less comfortable evidence. In her view 'collusion in stereotypical behaviours encourages women to maintain feelings of dependency and incompetence'. Clutterbuck[10] gives a useful review of the particular problems of male/female mentoring.

You may wish to test your own position, and your organization's, on a number of the issues raised here about women managers.

Exercise

1 What are my beliefs about why there are proportionately fewer women managers than there are women at work?
2 What do I believe my organization's beliefs to be?
3 Does my organization have any clear policy about women managers, and procedures to implement those policies?
4 What is my view about the existence of differences between the way in which a woman manager and a male manager will work?
5 Are there different management development needs for women?
6 What is my view and practice on the provision of women-only groups?
7 Do women learn differently from men? If so in what way?

MULTINATIONAL NEEDS

There are three major aspects which make management development in multinational organizations different from those which have a single national base:

- *differences in national culture*, with consequent differences, required styles and behaviours of managers
- *mixed management teams*, which require the effective integration of different cultures and styles
- *different management development systems*, involving a recognition that a system which works in one country may not work at all or in certain respects in another

The major work of practical value on cultural issues in management development is still Hofstede.[11] Because his research was conducted in one major organization with a strong managerial culture, the differences in national style that he drew out were identifiably national rather than influenced by organizational structure, techniques or processes. Hofstede described culture as 'a collective programming of the mind'. In his research he found that value patterns differed along four main dimensions:

- large or small power distance
- strong or weak uncertainty avoidance
- individualism versus collectivism
- masculinity versus femininity

The details of his definitions of these dimensions, and the attribution of them to particular countries, can be found in his book. We need only note here that he provides a research-based process for enabling managers to move beyond simply recognizing that people from other countries are different – and because they are different necessarily inferior or less effective! Working abroad, or working in your own country with managers from other countries, creates culture shock because your expectation of the right way of doing things differs from those of other countries. Those difficulties are, of course, exacerbated by language. The old joke about the United States and England being countries separated by a common language has the major merit of reminding us that it is all too easy to believe that another person has understood you. When the other person's language is not English, the difficulties that arise are often clearer, although equally the subject of horror stories and jokes.

The ethics of managers are another aspect of cultural belief. Some years ago I took part in a television programme and was fascinated to see how British-based managers attempted to defend the operation of different ethical practices outside the UK as compared from those they would use at home. An interesting analysis of this kind of issue occurred on some courses run for the Swedish company SAS. Participants were asked to list the values most important to them. An overwhelming majority of Swedish participants chose honesty as the most important; the value of honesty was not mentioned in the top fifteen by North American participants. Instead they listed competition, liberty and freedom. Competition is not an important value for Swedish managers or for Japanese managers. Different views about such issues were also found in Weinshall and Raveh.[12] Even more explicitly, they found that, in a case study about management failure, 2 per cent of French managers said 'fire him'; but 80 per cent of the American managers offered this solution.

The research studies here are important not least because they sometimes contradict stereotypes or perhaps provide clarification of the existence of a stereotype. As throughout this book, however, it is necessary to warn against generalization. Of course the casual informality of many American managers demonstrates the truth of a stereotype: but informality in personal relationships does not necessarily go with informality in communication within the managerial hierarchy. In a study I did of German and English managers, one group complained that the other was far too bound by rules of precedent and hierarchy. The British managers were astonished to find that it was the Germans who were making this complaint about them!

The question of the tightness of structure and responsibility, and the degree of openness in managerial relationships, is especially important in management development. Many UK and American books nowadays advocate much looser managerial relationships and concepts of teamwork which other countries, particularly in Asia and Africa, find quite bewildering and unusable.

It is therefore a major problem to adapt to the culture of a country when you are the expatriate manager. It is additionally difficult to manage cross-cultural relationships when you are participating in a mixed team of managers from several different cultures. I have worked with an American director working in England for an American multinational. Members of his team were predominantly British, but he also had several Germans, two other Americans and one solitary Frenchman. It so happened that he was extremely competent and flexible in his way of dealing with people; but even he had problems in trying to adapt his approach to the differing demands not merely of individuals, but of individuals with quite strong national characteristics. These factors affect the design and implementation of management development systems and influence perceptions about that implementation.

The comments about different cultures and management styles is significant for the design of systems. An appraisal scheme built on free and open exchange, including self-appraisal, may be well accepted in the United States, partially accepted in the United Kingdom and not accepted at all in some other countries. There has further been a major change in the patterns of job movement. The opportunities that used to exist in multinationals to send people abroad for a desirable period of experience in other countries is now much reduced. Understandably many countries prefer, and need, to develop their own managers instead of creating vacancies for managers from the parent organization. Desirable as it is that other countries should look after their own needs, this has substantially reduced certain kinds of management development opportunity for people from the parent company. An unfortunate consequence of this is that parent company senior managers may increasingly have had only visiting experience of the countries for which they may have senior responsibility at corporate headquarters. As Laurent[13] has shown, perceptions about careers and what it takes to develop careers may differ. American managers relate career to 'ambition and drive', while French managers see it as 'being labelled as having high potential'.

From a systematic management development point of view it may well be that the opportunities for posting abroad are diminishing at exactly the time when there is greater understanding of what needs to be done in order to make for a successful management appointment abroad! The advantages of distance and greater automomy, which in many respects provide a good test of management competence, have to be balanced against the more solitary and isolated nature of the manager's work. There may well be greater risks, both political and commercial, involved in working abroad. And domestic problems can contribute to failure at least as often as they contribute to success. There is also the re-entry difficulty, which is now more problematic than it is for spacecraft. Finding the right slot at the right time for the returning manager, or even promising to do so before his departure abroad, can cause major headaches.

The main problem is the ethnocentric view of the world, held in the corporate headquarters of a multinational in the UK. It is not only that other countries and other cultures may respond negatively to the UK style. They may well have a substantially different view of appropriate management development practices. It is true that some British managers are as tired of hearing about the more effective Japanese practices as their predecessors were of hearing about the United States in the 1960s. It so happens that the Japanese processes described by Handy[14] are very close to the Type 2 processes described in this book. However his report also helpfully describes practices in France, West Germany and the United States, and is clearly an important source for any adviser in a multinational.

There is one further aspect of cultural differences to be discussed. We have yet to see in the UK the evolution of managers from minority ethnic groups. In proportion to the population they are fewer than women, who have already started on the journey which will lead out of the ghetto. The main steps taken by ethnic minorities seem so far to have been into local government rather than in industry or commerce. Cheap laughs are available to anyone on the occasional excesses of programmes on anti-racism. But the issue cannot be laughed away, since it involves ethics and/or the allocation of managerial resources.

GRADUATES

A number of organizations recruit graduates primarily to fill immediate technical or functional needs. After time, experience, and achieved performance they merge into the totality of the unit they have joined and their development as managers follows the normal path for that organization.

Other organizations recruit graduates less for such immediate technical or functional purposes than to create a pool of intelligent people with high potential as a means of providing for management of the future. The difference in objectives and immediate location for these two different kinds of graduate recruitment illustrates the problems that arise. Whereas the first group go into a proper job, although admittedly it may be below their intellectual level or ambition, the latter group often go into no clear functional stream.

The problems experienced by management trainees over the years recur, although they do seem to have diminished since the awful days of the 1950s. The problem of the Cook's tour, where graduates were hurtled around a number of departments for a few weeks or months at a time with no proper job at any staging point, were well known by the early 1960s. Few organizations now fall into that trap. More frequently organizations will put graduates or management trainees into departments for more substantial periods, or will employ them on specific tasks or projects. Not only is this something which intelligent graduates now demand, but it is something which organizations themselves have come to recognize as necessary if they are to make any judgement about the actual capacity of the graduates recruited.

There is no mystery about what to do with graduates. There needs to be a formal development programme for them which will include appropriate courses, they need to have assignments in particular units or departments long enough to establish that they have done a definable piece of work. If sharp distinctions are made between themselves and others of equivalent age but with no degree the expectations and motivation of non-degree people will be reduced.

Of course one of the prime issues here is the same as for more experienced managers: whether the process of learning from the experiences offered to graduate entrants is actually effective in learning terms. Barrington's book[15] is an excellent guide to some aspects of this whole graduate training process, precisely because it focuses on issues about learning and not simply on issues about moving people between jobs.

Reference was made in Chapter 8 to MBAs. Some stereotypical thinking about MBA recruits has become firmly entrenched in a number of organizations. They are seen as expensive recruits who want to do the managing director's job before they have shown that they can manage a department. They are characterized as arrogant, as possessing intellectual and analytical skills rather than the practical skills on which so much effective management is believed to be based. Of course, if all organizations believed this then no business school would be able to run a traditional MBA programme. So the traditional picture is partial rather than complete. (Although some criticisms of the content and learning processes of traditional programmes are valid.) Current developments in MBA programmes all emphasize relevance and reality, whether they be the City University programme based around competencies or the IMC programme based on action learning. It does seem likely that the associated development of programmes which focus on particular organizational needs, whether on a consortium basis or an individual organization, will provide both greater demands and greater opportunities for effective management development. There is undoubtedly a group of young managers who want the discipline and structure of a formal MBA, but who also want it conducted in terms of more appropriate general management processes and more specific relevance to their own organization. The future growth of MBA programmes is more likely in this area than in that of providing open programmes offering a career break to middle managers.

REFERENCES

1   ROBERTS T. *Developing effective managers*. IPM, 1974
2   TRAINING SURVEY UNIT. *Survey on management training and development*. Department of Employment, 1971
3   FRAKER S. 'Why women aren't getting to the top'. *Fortune Magazine*. April 1984
4   MARSHALL J. 'Women managers'. In Mumford A, *A handbook of management development*. Gower, 1991
5   SIMMONS M. 'Undoing men's gender conditioning'. *Industrial and Commercial Training*. November 1986
6   ALBAN METCALFE B. *Career development of British managers*. British Institute of Management, 1984
7   KOLB D. *Experiential learning*. Prentice Hall, 1984

8   BOWEY D. 'Were men meant to mentor women?' *Training and Development*. February, 1985
9   KRAM K. 'Phases of the mentor relationship'. *Academy of Management Journal*. Vol 16, No 4, 1983
10 CLUTTERBUCK D. *Everyone needs a mentor*. 2nd ed. IPM, 1991
11 HOFSTEDE G. *Culture's consequences*. Sage, 1980
12 WEINSHALL T. D. and RAVEH Y. A. *Managing growing organisations*. Wiley, 1983
13 LAURENT A. 'The cross cultural puzzle'. *Human Resource Management*. Vol 25, No 1, Spring 1986
14 HANDY C. *Making managers*. NEDO, 1987
15 BARRINGTON A. *Learning about management*. McGraw Hill, 1985

11 Continuous Learning and Development

We have examined the reality behind the management cliche 'I learned from experience'. Another cliche might almost have been invented specifically about learning: 'you can take a horse to water but you cannot make it drink'. The provision of a greater range of opportunities, and indeed the generation of a greater awareness of the opportunities to learn from real management experiences, may turn out to be rather like taking the horse to water. Those of us guiding the horse may be very well aware that we are offering splendid refreshment; if the horse does not want water but oats then we have both had a wasted journey. This chapter is concerned with how to help managers not only recognize but make better use of formal and informal opportunities for learning. The wide variety of influences on learning is indicated in Figure. 11.1

THE EXPERIENCE OF THE READER SO FAR

The introduction offered readers options about the sequence in which chapters might be read. The options were based on a view about the possible preferences of readers for particular aspects of management development. That was a small-scale attempt to recognize individually different needs. The book has also attempted to demonstrate the learning cycle illustrated in Chapter 2. Most of the books and articles I have read about management development essentially concentrate on the final two stages of that cycle:

Figure 11.1   Influences on Learning

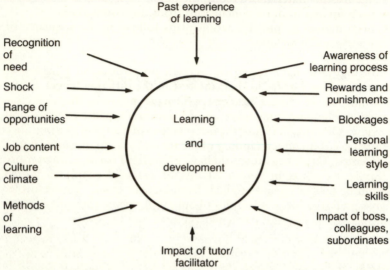

- a statement of the author's conclusions
- a series of statements of practical things to do, with the suggestion that the reader should plan action on them.

There are practical workbooks which give individuals practical exercises in various aspects of developing themselves. Pedler *et al.*[1] is an excellent and widely used example of this.

It seemed to me necessary that this book should attempt to cover the whole learning cycle. The introduction of practical exercises at various stages in each of the chapters was intended to meet two objectives:

- to give readers the opportunity to test out the propositions and statements against their own experience and beliefs
- to provide a practical demonstration of the application of the learning cycle to reading the book – a learning experience

So in each chapter readers:

- have had the particular experience of reading the book
- reviewed the information they have about their personal approach to management development, and that of their organiz-

ation. They have then been able to compare those experiences against the material offered in the book
- been invited to draw conclusions from this comparison
- been invited to prepare action plans following the sequence of review and conclude

You may also have tested the second proposition in Chapter 2, that individuals differ in their interest in the different stages of the learning cycle. Some readers will have enjoyed the exercises precisely because they give opportunities to pause, reflect and review. Others will regard the intervention of exercises as a nuisance which holds up understanding of the mental system or model being presented. Others again would have preferred a balance much more heavily weighted in favour of lots of practical examples which could be picked up and applied. Such readers would, for example, have preferred more examples of appraisal forms, succession plans and more examples of particular types of training course.

The stage we have now reached is that of helping to make some readers more aware of some of the reasons for their reactions to the book. The result of that increased awareness will, it is hoped, be not only an improved ability on the part of the reader to understand her or his own reactions, but an understanding of the different reactions of people with different learning styles. This book itself is potentially a proof of the theme of individuality which it has so strongly emphasized.

THEORIES OF LEARNING

It is predictable in terms of learning styles that some readers will want more evidence about the basis for the statements about Learning Processes made so far. Those who do want this should look at the work of three people. Malcolm Knowles[2] has had a major influence on people who are interested in adult learning. His model of the learner is that:

- the learner is self directed but has a conditioned expectation to be dependent and to be taught
- the learner comes with experience which means that, for many kinds of learning, adults are themselves the richest resources for one another and that there is a wide range of experience in most groups of learners

- people are ready to learn when they have a need to perform more effectively in some aspect of their lives
- for the most part adults do not learn for the sake of learning. They learn in order to be able to perform a task, solve a problem, or live in a more satisfying way

The work of Reg Revans and his definition of action learning were summarized in Chapter 2. He has contributed two theoretical statements. The first he described as 'System Beta', which involves the assembly of data, the development of a theory, experimentation, the comparison of results derived from experiment and the final evaluation of the theory. This theory stems from his scientific background and will be seen to strongly resemble the learning cycles proposed by Kolb, and Honey and Mumford. The other major aspect of his theory is the one which has really generated action learning. Revans identified a difference between what he described as 'programmed knowledge' and the 'questioning approach'. Programmed knowledge (P) is learning from what somebody else has learned, this information being provided in the form of books, papers, studies and lectures. Questioning (Q) is learning from your own processes of action and reflection. This latter process is called action learning.

David Kolb's contribution[3] was first in the design of his version of the learning cycle, which is still used by some management educators and trainers. Its original neat representation was supplemented by his major theoretical contribution, which was that of translating the relatively common acceptance that 'people learn differently' into the concepts of different learning styles, each related to a stage on the cycle.

Is an understanding of, and a commitment to, some theory of learning necessary for effective management development? As far as many managers are concerned, clearly not. Some, who score highly on the Theorist style (or as abstract conceptualizers on the Kolb model), would probably want this sort of background if they were being introduced to their own learning processes. A significant number of them, however, would not miss an explanation of the theory, simple though it is. They would be much more concerned with the practical implications and applications. The point is more arguable for management development advisers, educators and trainers. They too will have preferences in terms of learning process. But as people giving advice on, and constructing events involving, conscious learning they must surely have at least the small degree of theoretical knowledge offered here.

Exercise

1 What is your reaction to the statements about learning theory given above?
2 How do your practices relate if at all to these theories?
3 Do these statements help to explain your personal experiences of learning?
4 Do they help you to analyse and understand what is being offered by other management developers, educators and trainers?

THE APPLICATION OF LEARNING THEORY AND LEARNING STYLES

The effective use of learning opportunities depends on a conscious attempt to improve the design of the opportunities on the one hand, and the understanding of the learner about learning processes and skills on the other. This means working through a diagnostic instrument, or alternatively through a structured exercise of some kind as giving learners a better understanding of their own learning processes. The early exercises in Chapter 1 are one version of this. Some advisers prefer not to work through the formal categories of learning styles, regarding these as potentially inhibiting. The arguments for and against explicitness are set out in Mumford.[4] (Kolb's work has already been mentioned.) The Honey and Mumford *Manual of learning styles*[5] shows how specific material about individual learning preferences can be used for the following purposes:

- helping individuals to review their approach to learning, to select opportunities related to their preference, and for some, progress to building learning skills outside their existing preference
- for the general design of courses so that they take account of different learning styles more effectively
- for the specific design of particular events to meet any proponderant needs that may exist, which may mean designing an event to take account of any particular majority preference. If through the LSQ you know you are going to encounter majority preference for the Activist style, you should design the event differently from the way you would design an event where you find you have a majority of Theorists

- the better design of on the job learning opportunities in relation to individual preferences. For example, there is little point in throwing somebody in to observe another manager at work if the observer is very low on the Reflector score

It should be emphasized that the prospective power of these diagnostic processes is not only to improve the capacity of the designer of learning experiences. It is to enable the learner to understand his or her own learning processes, not only in relation to that particular event, but for future learning opportunities.[6] It ought to be a major imperative that such processes are built in to many of our formal learning events. Not only is it our responsibility to help managers to learn better during those events, but we ought to be helping them to learn more effectively outside them. It is a sad commentary on some major management education programmes that no such attempt is made. Apparently the priorities of many business schools and training centres relate entirely to traditional management skills or functional knowledge, not at all to the skills of learning which are actually required in order to improve those skills and that knowledge!

OTHER INFLUENCES ON LEARNING

Individual learning preferences are clearly not the only influence on whether somebody learns from a particular opportunity. Figure 11.1 shows a number of other influences. Again it seems important that we not only identify that these influences exist, but help individuals to recognize and perhaps cope with them. Some work by Temporal and Boydell,[7] and by Stuart[8] helps to define some of the problems. Honey and Mumford have now put together a manual which assists individuals to review their own understanding of learning opportunities and diagnoses their likely ability or willingess to take advantage of them.[9] The manual includes a complementary tool for the Learning Styles Questionnaire, a Learning Diagnostic Questionnaire. This enables individuals to assess themselves on:

- their knowledge and skills in learning
- their working situation
- their attitudes and emotions

While primarily intended as an individual tool, the working

situation element of the questionnaire can be used by groups or complete organizations. Answers to the question under this heading will provide a view of the extent to which the group or the organization as a whole is seen as positively inclined, or negatively antipathetic, to learning.

A combination of the Learning Styles Questionnaire and the Learning Diagnostic Questionnaire can therefore give individuals powerful and useful feedback on the reasons why they approach learning in the way they do. When they are faced with a structured learning experience, such as a course, having this information at least generates better understanding of how they are going to react and perhaps enables them to make more enlightened choices between such experiences. However, the majority of learning experiences are not created and structured in that way. They are the informal and accidental experiences that provide partial and inefficient learning, or they are the improved version of this which I have called Type 2. One feature of managerial experience as a learning process is that since the major element is the management experience, and not learning, the manager has less choice. The manager can reject a course but he cannot put aside a task, a project or a meeting. The manager may have no choice about the managerial experience; but failure to learn from it satisfactorily is not the result of deliberate and conscious avoidance but simply a failure to recognize the opportunity or ignorance about how to learn from it most effectively.

Most such opportunities are seen and used in retrospect: a manager looks back on a particularly powerful managerial experience and more or less consciously registers learning from it. Improving the informal and accidental processes requires a better understanding of what managers actually do when they say they 'learn from experience'. In our further research with directors we established that while most of them learn by looking back over events consciously, the extent and depth of such reviewing varied. There were circumstances in which learning was thought about in advance, as a prospective experience, or where learning could be envisaged as arising from a future managerial activity. We identified the four different approaches to learning from on the job experiences as follows:

- *intuitive*, where managers learn, but unconsciously from experience. Learning occurs through some natural process of osmosis. 'I suspect you are doing it all the time without realizing you are doing so.'

- *incidental*, where learning emerges by chance from activities that jolt managers into conducting a post mortem. Difficulties, mishaps and frustrations often provide the spur for the incidental learner. In such circumstances learning is conscious but it happens in an unstructured, informal way. 'It is the originality of the experience that makes me think about what I've got from it.'
- *retrospective*, where learning occurs much more consciously by thinking about what has happened and reaching conclusions. In addition to the mishaps and mistakes from which the incidental learner learns, retrospective learners are more inclined to draw lessons from routine events and successes. The conscious process involves thinking things through in the head, in conversation and sometimes on paper. 'Reviewing is essential to put things into perspective.'
- *prospective*, involving planning to learn before an experience. This means seeing future events not merely as management requirements, but as events from which it is possible to learn. 'Sorting out what you want to get in advance increases your chances of getting something worthwhile.' Of course the prospective approach is then combined with the retrospective, since the effective learner later reviews what he or she has actually learned from the experience identified in advance.

The four approaches are not mutually exclusive. We have found that some managers more characteristically learn from one approach in preference to another; but most carry out at least the first three. Managers can make more effective use of learning opportunities by being helped to expand their recognition of opportunities and identification of learning processes. The powerful process of completing a learning log, increasingly advocated and used in management development, is found by a number of managers to be unreal and therefore unusable. Those particularly geared to the retrospective and prospective approach keep such a log; but others will not. For this latter group it is much more sensible to propose processes which gear themselves to existing managerial processes, like adding a few notes to a list of work activities or to a weekly summary of priorities. These ideas are further developed in a booklet written for directors but of value also for managers.[10]

LIFE-LONG LEARNING

The need for individuals to learn and develop throughout their working life has become a cliché. Whereas twenty or thirty years ago managers might have presumed that they were in relatively stable jobs which required familiar skills, this is today much less true for most managers. Indeed, the idea of a 'career' in management presumes that people will move from one job to another, which will obviously require additional knowledge and skills. The career may be achieved in a single organization, and have an unchanged focus, or it may be achieved through several organizations. The manager's eventual destination may be clear at the outset or be the result of a series of changed decisions about appropriate focus – a zig-zag rather than steady upward movement on a graph. The zig-zags may represent changes of focus – a move from one function to another, from one size or type of organization to another, from one view of a desired destination ('I want to get to the top') to another ('I want a fulfilling job which enables me to spend time with my family').

The organizational input to career choice is made through the processes described in Chapters 4–6. But a great deal of formal career planning necessarily assumes a substantial element of a steady-state organization. But the career that is on offer through the planned process may not be available when the time comes to put the plan into effect. Most dramatically, an organization may cease to exist because it goes out of business. In less dramatic form mergers or acquisitions may affect the availability of particular jobs. It is therefore absolutely appropriate that we should emphasize life-long learning as a major theme in management development.

CAREER DEVELOPMENT

Some organizations attempt to plan careers; life provides opportunities; and individuals choose what they want to be. It is the interaction of these three which creates careers. Schein[11] has given by far the best analysis of this interaction. He describes an individual's 'career anchor' as consisting of:

- self-perceived talents and abilities
- self-perceived motives and needs
- self-perceived attitudes and values

The career anchor emphasizes evolution, development and discovery through actual experience. It is the result of an early interaction between the individual and the work environment. Characteristically career anchors involve:

- technical or functional competence
- managerial competence, especially the ability to analyse and solve problems, interpersonal skills and emotional competence
- security and stability
- creativity
- autonomy and independence

Schein's book also includes a self-analysis form enabling individuals to identify their own position. A book by Francis[12] provides a greater variety of suggestions, checklists and questionnaires, and is very much a workbook rather than the analytical model that Schein's is.

Paul Evans has contributed to our understanding of two different aspects of career development. With his colleague Bartolome he looked at the impact of career choices on home life. They particularly showed that it is the feelings generated by work that determine the quality of private life. In their view problems were caused by inappropriate, random and ill considered processes for selecting and developing careers.[13] More recently, Evans has suggested that careers should not be seen as purely hierarchical processes, but that managers and organizations should think more of opportunities for steady-state or spiral careers.[14] He argues that there are three stages in patterns of concern in career development:

- *exploration*, particularly when young (Evans suggests this is a time for self-discovery and that too much planning is neither feasible nor desirable)
- *establishment*, the stage at which people become fully aware of what they want to be (as a result of the opportunities they have taken at the exploration stage)
- *mid–late career phase*, in which being on a plateau does not necessarily equate with less development

SELF-DEVELOPMENT

Action learning and self-development merged as major concepts in management development in the 1970s, and have some features in common. Behind Revans's insistence that managers learn most effectively by working on their own real problems is a resistance to the idea of the formal tutor. Self-development took on board the growing awareness that management development was not effective when it was a process 'done to' a manager. The view of a manager as a passive recipient of processes which other people had designed, according to needs which had not been established with the individual (if indeed they had been established at all), was recognizably one cause of failure in management development.

The main authors who have identified the meaning of, and the processes involved in, self-development have been Pedler, Burgoyne and Boydell. Their first book, essentially a workbook, has deservedly gone into a second edition.[15] In this they define self-development as 'personal development, with a manager taking primary responsibility for his own learning and for choosing the means to achieve this'. They define a large part of the difference as being to do with treating managers as agents in their own development processes, rather than patients receiving treatment from experts. As shown earlier, they also distinguish between learning and development, and they are especially concerned with the development of the whole person, rather than with discrete, job-centred aspects of learning.

Self-development is not an activity analogous to particular techniques like role plays, case studies or lectures. Nor is it simply a collection of relatively untraditional approaches to learning through biography, self-assessment, questionnaires, development workshops or counselling. Self-development represents a dramatically fundamental and difficult shift of thinking in that:

- Responsibility for learning is taken on by the learner, and not seen as the responsibility of the provider of learning opportunities.
- The focus is on the individual and his or her particular needs rather than on large groups of managers with general needs.
- The manager is not simply the recipient of judgements by other people on his or her learning needs and their solutions, but is rather involved in the analysis of the needs and the discussion of solutions.
- Because of the process of involvement, responsibility clearly rests with the learner, leaving fewer excuses to complain about lack of relevance or inapplicability of solutions to supposed needs.
- The combination of involvement and responsibility generates

commitment to personal action, instead of acceptance of the
need to follow someone else's prescription.
- Because individuals work on defining their own personal needs
  they have already begun to engage in not only the generation of
  solutions but work on the solutions. The sometimes unhelpful
  distinction between analysis and action is reduced.
- While all of the reasons offered so far can be seen as pragmatic
  statements of how to secure more effective individual management development, an even more fundamental issue at least
  whispers in the background and occasionally shouts in the
  foreground. The more we insist that managers are responsible
  for their own development, the more we also imply that they
  have the right to choose not only pragmatically but also ethically.
  This closely relates to the associated point of whether we are
  developing or seeking to develop the whole person, or are
  operating at more immediate managerial levels of particular
  skills.

Just as most managers are not astonished to read that learning
from experience is important, necessary and underemphasized in
management development, so they are not at all surprised to be
told that they are responsible for their own development. Whatever
the contribution they recognize may be made by a relatively
benevolent employing organization, most of them would recognize
that 'when you come down to it, my development is really up to
me'. The philosophy of self-development fits very well with other
ideas already identified in this book. A process which helps
managers to see that they can define and use their own opportunities,
instead of being responsive to someone else's identification and
provision of opportunities, is entirely in tune with one of the major
themes of this book.

     However, many self-development processes focus on off-the-
job activities and seem less concerned than I would think desirable
with issues of how to carry learning forward into the real world.
There has been a concentration on the assessment of needs through
self-development processes such as a workbook, a workshop, an
assessment centre, or individual counselling. The range of such
activities is well set out in two collections of articles.[16] The later
collection is particularly interesting in terms of the themes of this
chapter, because it gives much more emphasis than earlier works
to the central significance of how a manager learns. Much of the
earlier literature fell into the error of supposing that learning would
naturally be enhanced by self-development.

The major omissions in the literature are suggestions about how to decide which processes will best meet the objectives of self-development. As always, the temptation is for the people designing the process to propose that things are done in the way which the designer finds most comfortable. I am optimistic that most managers can engage successfully in some kind of self-development process; but it is still clear that spraying all managers with the same holy water is unlikely to be successful. The willingness to engage in some degree of self-analysis is essential if you are to engage in self-development. This does not extend to a necessary acceptance by every individual of exactly the same kind of process through which to engage in that self-analysis. My own experience, operating mainly on issues of job effectiveness rather than the whole person, has been that I have been much too optimistic over the years about how far managers are prepared to go in learning about themselves and about group processes.

Finally, there is the continuing problem of taking self-development as a philosophy and as a collection of processes back into the organization. It is wrong to design and run self-development activities which do not devote a very substantial proportion of energy to the identification of the positive and negative contributions made by the boss and the general working environment.

The other major issue of difficulty is that of the role of the adviser. The idea of giving up the role of expert tutor and direct leader of learning in favour of being a facilitator of other people's learning is not one which all management development advisers can manage or accept.

It would be wrong to leave this major topic with an expression of reservation and uncertainties. Pedler *et al.*[16] show that there are problems of definition for precisely the reasons which also make the philosophy attractive. They ask whether self-development groups and distance learning for a higher degree are really part of the same philosopy. The fact that the words have been stretched in this way is probably a compliment to the essential idea, although worrying in terms of clarity. The idea of managers choosing to meet their own needs in their own way is entirely correct. Enabling them to do so successfully has very much been a theme of this book. (A more extensive review of materials on this very important field is given in Further Reading.)

USING OTHERS TO HELP

Chapter 9 spelled out the variety of people and the variety of organizational and personal responsibilities involved in helping an individual to learn. This section concentrates on the ways in which other people can help on the job. The people involved are identified in Figure 11.2. An excellent description of the kind of activities involved is given by Stuart.[17] As he points out one of the most useful steps is actually to draw up a map showing the people who may be able to help, identify which are already being used, and which are not. As Stuart shows, individuals may help in three primary ways:

- clearing the way for learning
- tooling up for learning
- direct learning interventions

The primary issue is probably the extent to which any individual manager is able to make his or her learning needs and strategies clear to others. One of the ways in which formal training and educational processes can help is in giving people explicit experience of this. I frequently use pairs and trios on management courses for this purpose. This is not only helpful in the immediate sense of developing learning plans, it is also helpful in giving people experience in a relatively supportive environment of the process of sharing and developing plans. It is possible to extend the whole process to the full group in an off-the-job situation, and this is an option particularly likely to be available in an action learning set or a self-development group. As Stuart points out, one of the issues is whether individuals look for help from others who have similar learning styles, or whether they use others to compensate for their preferences. It is one of the achieved benefits of organized discussion of learning styles and learning processes that individuals, pairs and groups can use each others' strengths and compensate each other for weaknesses.

One of the prime sources of help ought, of course, to be the boss. For reasons indicated in Chapter 9, this is easier to state than it is to achieve. It will undoubtedly be the boss who has the greatest input on the effective conversion of Type 1 into Type 2 learning experiences. It is the boss who knows what kind of managerial activities a subordinate will be involved or has been involved in, and who can encourage the subordinate to engage in the reviewing processes indicated earlier in this chapter. The process of shared

Figure 11.2 Interaction in Learning

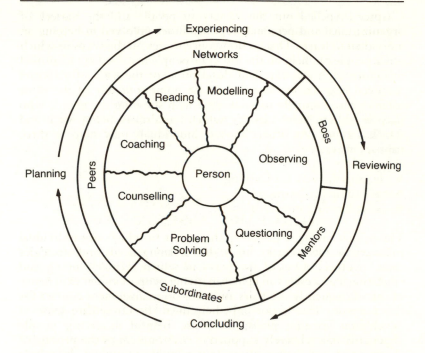

problem solving, for example, is a prime source of potential learning. Naturally it is most comfortable for the subordinate if the boss takes the initiative in using such experiences to assess or confirm learning; but it may be necessary for the subordinate to take the initiative in seeking such a review. The prime issue is stimulating an awareness of learning opportunities arising from real-work experiences, and then creating a discussion of those experiences.

THE LEARNING ORGANIZATION

Readers have been introduced to the impact of the organization on individual learning in earlier chapters. Definitions of an understanding about what is meant by the learning organization have not yet achieved great clarity. Pedler and his colleagues are again leading the way here, and say that it is 'an organisation which facilitates the learning of all its members and continuously transforms itself'.[18] Chris Argyris has described organizational learning, but not the learning organization. An article by Beck[19] reviews current experience (mainly in the United States). At the present time it does seem difficult to establish that such organizations are doing more than effectively combining good formal processes of management development with some kind of encouragement of on-the-job development. 'The learning organization' is an attractive phrase and one which potentially combines many of the ideas expressed in this book, but it is not yet evident that there is any substantial practice to support the potential.

CONTINUOUS LEARNING AND ACADEMIC ASSESSMENT

The crucial relevance of direct work experience as an academically valid part of formal training and education is being increasingly recognized. The idea of basing a management qualification purely on traditional forms of academic education is now seen as unhelpful. The idea of assessing experience developed first in the United States as a means of opening up entry to academic courses; it is now being developed into a process by which appropriate current experiences are built into qualification programmes. Innovative work in this country has largely been led by Norman Evans, now Director of the Learning from Experience Trust. A succinct summary of the issues involved in assessing experience before entry to a programme is given in his article.[20] This idea, particularly when continued within a qualification programme, represents a major shift of emphasis towards reality. It also reinforces a point frequently made during this book. If people are to be asked to review their past experience and what they have learned from it, then they need to understand the learning process in which they have been involved, and to have some structure for reporting on it. The provision of such a structure is not, however, primarily going to give better results in terms of achieved literacy about learning. It will bring about a transformation in the *actuality* of learning. My own institution gives explicit encouragement to precisely this process. We require that people who have completed our MBA programme should, five years after graduation, show that they have continued to learn during that period. Thus the practice of learning is built into their continued membership of our institution which they will have acquired initially with their MBA.

Exercise

1 What processes do we currently use to help managers understand and develop their learning processes?
2 Which of the ideas in this chapter might we pick up and use, for which purposes?
3 Does our organization,and the processes it offers, concentrate on the formal training input or is it also concerned with an effective learning environment on the job?
4 Which of the influences on learning given in Figure 11.1 score highest in my own experience?
5 Taking an overall view of the organization, which influence is most important?

NOT AN END BUT A BEGINNING

So we finish where we started in chapter 1 – with the recording of learning experiences, brought about by questions designed to elicit the nature and results of that learning. We also finish with the statement of things that have occurred as a result of a process – work – rather than with a statement about inputs. I hope that readers will by now be fully convinced that management development is indeed about learning.

REFERENCES

1 PEDLER M., BURGOYNE J. and BOYDELL T. *A manager's guide to self development*. 2nd ed. McGraw Hill, 1986
2 KNOWLES M. *Andragogy in action*. Jossey Bass, 1985
3 KOLB D. *Experiential learning*. Prentice Hall, 1984
4 MUMFORD A. 'Learning to learn for managers'. *Journal of European Industrial Training*. Vol 10, No 2, 1986
5 HONEY P. and MUMFORD A. *Manual of learning styles*. 3rd ed. Honey, 1992
6 HONEY P. and MUMFORD A. *Using your learning styles*. Honey, 1986
7 TEMPORAL P. and BOYDELL T. *Helping managers to learn*. Sheffield City Polytechnic, 1981

8 STUART R. 'Maximizing managers' day to day learning', in Cox C. and Beck J. *Management development: advances in theory and practice.* Wiley, 1984; and 'Using others to learn', in MUMFORD A. (ed.), *Handbook of Management Development.* Gower, 1986

9 HONEY P. and MUMFORD A. *Manual of learning opportunities.* Honey, 1989

10 MUMFORD A., HONEY P. and ROBINSON G. *Developing directors: using experience.* Institute of Directors, 1989

11 SCHEIN E. *Career dynamics.* Addison Wesley, 1978

12 FRANCIS D. *Managing your own career.* Fontana, 1985

13 EVANS P. and BARTOLOME F. *Must success cost so much?* Grant McIntyre, 1980

14 EVANS N. 'New directions in career management'. *Personnel Management*, 1986

15 PEDLER, BURGOYNE & BOYDELL, *op cit*

16 BOYDELL T. and PEDLER M., eds. *Management self development.* Gower, 1981 and PEDLER M., BURGOYNE J. and BOYDELL T., eds. *Applying self development in organisations.* Prentice Hall, 1988

17 STUART R. 'Using others to learn'. In MUMFORD A. (ed), *Handbook of management development.* Gower, 1986

18 PEDLER M., BOYDELL T. and BURGOYNE J. 'Towards the learning company'. *Management Education and Development* Vol. 20, Part 1, 1989.

19 BECK M. 'Learning organisations'. *Industrial and Commercial Training*, March 1989

20 EVANS R. 'Assessing prior experiential learning'. *Industrial and Commercial Training.* January 1989

12 Additional Resources and Further Reading

INSTITUTIONS

Association for Management Education and Development
77 Oxford Street
London W1R 1RB

This body draws together management educators, management developers and trainers in organizations, and training consultancies.

European Women's Management Development Network
Rue Washington 40
B1050 Brussels Belgium

or

Ashridge Management College
Berkhamsted
Hertfordshire HP4 1NS

This forum gives special voice to women and women's issues.

International Foundation for Action Learning
64 Northchurch Road
London N1 3NY

This small group spreads the message of action learning.

Institute of Personnel Management
Camp Road
Wimbledon
London SW19 4UW

This professional association not only provides literature, as this book attests, but provides through its national and regional conferences and branch meetings further opportunities to discuss management development issues.

Institute of Training and Development
Marlow House
Marlow
Buckinghamshire SL7 1BN

Like the IPM but on a smaller and perhaps less intense scale, this group offers opportunities for the discussion of management development issues.

European Foundation for Management Development
Rue Washington 40
B1050 Brussels, Belgium

This organization draws together consultants, in-company advisers and management educators from the whole of Europe. It has a particularly strong emphasis on and membership in business schools.

Training Agency

Moorfoot
Sheffield
S1 4PQ

In different manifestations under different titles, and apparently constantly subject to changes of priority and strategy as directed by government, the Training Agency gallantly soldiers on. It has sponsored some excellent work in the management development area and is a useful source of advice. It has published a catalogue of its projects and publications in the management development field. Both advice and catalogue can be obtained from the address above.

The Management Charter Initiative/National Forum for Management Education and Development

As mentioned in the text one of the most useful results of Charles Handy's report was the development of the Management Charter Initiative and its code of practice. At the time of writing the attempt of what started as the Council for Management Education and Development to introduce formal management qualifications based on assessed competencies has shuddered to a halt. There are sharply differing views on whether this is or is not a good thing. In any event management developers should certainly check out their position on the Management Charter initiative. This can be done by contacting the National Forum, the address of which is in some doubt at the time of publication.

SUPPLIERS OF CONSULTANCY AND RESOURCES

It is really necessary to turn to specific reference books in order to find what you might need here.

Mike Abrahams has written a very useful guide to the choice of consultants in *Handbook of management development*, edited by A. Mumford. Gower, 1986.

Specific reference books include *AMED directory of consultants* and *Trainer resources*, published by Institute of Training and Development (see above).

A number of books describe particular processes such as films, case studies, business games. It is best to access the most recent of these by approaching the library of your professional institution. In addition to those mentioned above, the British Institute of Management (Management House, Cottingham Road, Corby, Northants NN17 1TT; telephone: 0536 204222) has a very good and helpful Library service, which can be used either by individual members or by individuals from member organizations.

The centre for the Study of Management Learning is part of the:

University of Lancaster
Lancaster LA1 4YX

This has been the one organization specifically dedicated to improved understanding of teaching and learning processes. It remains the central focus for a great deal of research and associated practical work. It publishes a newsletter and runs annual conferences.

National Training Index

25 Poland Street
London W1

This organization has for many years carried out an assessment of courses, largely by securing responses from consumers. The subscription cost can very easily and quickly be recovered by avoiding the cost of sending a manager on an inappropriately low level course.

JOURNALS

Personnel Management has the biggest circulation of any of the journals dealing with this field. Since it deals with the whole Personnel field articles on management development obviously do not come up every month.

MCB University Press based at Bradford has a number of specialist training and development journals, to which it adds regularly. I should 'declare an interest' in that I am at the time of writing editor of one of the journals mentioned below:

Journal of Management Development

Journal of European Industrial Training

Industrial and Commercial Training

Readers would be well advised to get the latest list of journals in this field by writing to MCB University Press at 62 Toller Lane, Bradford, West Yorkshire, BD8 9DY

FURTHER READING

The following comments are intended to indicate books or articles which I regard as of prime significance, or which offer a different view from the ones I have emphasized in the relevant chapters. Specific references given in the original chapters are not repeated here.

Chapters 1 and 2

The essential question here is what you consider an appropriate definition of management development. A comprehensive statement of the traditional view of management development will be found in *Management development in the organization*, by David Ashton and Mark Easterby-Smith, Macmillan, 1979. In terms of the argument presented here this is of particular interest because it claims to provide a comprehensive view of management development, but focuses entirely on the formal processes.

Christopher Molander, in *Management development*, Chartwell-Bratt, 1986, similarly focuses entirely on formal processes in his definition. His analysis of content, however, usefully brings out the possibility of three types of focus: individual, group, and organization.

This kind of analysis is taken much further by Robin Snell and Don Binsted in their *Issues in management development* published by CSML in 1985.

On action learning I chose to refer to the most usable of Revans's many writings. The whole field is surveyed in *Management bibliographies and reviews*, Vol 11, No 2, 1985, 'A review of action learning', by Alan Mumford. There have been two collections of articles on action learning:

M. Pedler, ed, *Action learning in practice*, 2nd ed, Gower, 1991

Journal of Management Development, Special Issue on Action Learning, Vol 6, No 2, 1987

Chapter 3

My own book *Developing top managers* is the most extensive study so far of how senior managers learn to do their jobs, and why informal processes are so paramount. The American book given below similarly focuses on real managerial experiences, and also shows why work-based experiences are so powerful. It does not, however, describe the learning process so well.

M. McCall, M. Lombardo and A. Morrison, *The lessons of experience*, Lexington, 1988.

The article by Stuart referred to in Chapter 3 is an excellent short and clear statement.

Chapter 4

The popularity and importance of the subject are indicated by the continuing stream of articles and books. The book by Randell remains the best general introduction; the book by Long is also fundamental. A thorough study of the subject would include the following books:

C. Fletcher and R. Williams, *Performance appraisal and career development*, Hutchinson, 1985

G. L. Morrisey, *Performance appraisals for business and industry*, Addison Wesley, 1984

A. Stewart and V. Stewart, *Practical performance appraisal*, Gower, 1977

A paper by Bill Braddick and Peter Smith of Ashridge Management College (Berkhamsted, Herts. HP4 1NS; telephone: 044284 3491), 'The design of appraisal systems', includes a most valuable review of the different purposes of different participants in appraisal. Although not referred to in this chapter, the work by Ed Schein quoted in Chapter 11, *Career dynamics*, should certainly be read.

The continuing interest in assessment centres is well demonstrated by the useful articles in a special issue of the *Journal of Management Development*, Vol 4, No 4, 1985.

Chapter 5

An alternative view to the one I have presented on levels of career development is given by:

C. Margerison, 'Achieving capacity and competency to manage', *Journal of Management Development*, Vol 4, No 3, 1985

The issue of plateaued managers is addressed in two articles:

Paul Evans, 'New directions in career management', *Personnel Management*, December 1986

For the career patterns and work attitudes of both plateaued and non-plateaued managers, see C. Orpen, *International Journal of Manpower*, Vol 4, No 4, 1983

Chapter 6

Business strategy is increasingly seen as a major cause and vehicle for management development. In addition to the articles quoted, it is worth looking at:

W. P. Nilsson, *Achieving goals through executive development*, Addison Wesley, 1987

This gives some useful insights on this particular issue, although it is overdominated by courses and with remarkably little to say about the development and learning processes associated.

David Hussey, *Management training and corporate strategy*, Pergamon Press, 1988

J. F. Bolt, 'Tailor executive development to strategy', *Harvard Business Review*, November 1985

A. Mayo, 'Business strategies and management development', *Industrial and Commercial Training*, March 1989

An Ashridge Research Project on *Management for the future*, published in 1987, presents some interesting views about likely changes in skill and competency requirements.

Chapter 7

The development issues arising from job moves, on which I have used Gabarro as my main source, are also usefully covered in:

Peter Smith, 'The stages in a manager's job', in V. Hammond, ed, *Current research in management*, Frances Pinter, 1985

C. Parker and Al Lewis, 'Beyond the Peter principle', *Journal of European Industrial Training*, Vol 5, No 6, 1981

The main works on action learning have been mentioned earlier. John

Morris, while coming from the same philosophical base, describes his own approaches very well in:

J. Morris, 'Joint development activities in practice', *Journal of Management Development*, Vol 1, No 3, 1982

The literature on mentors is largely covered in the book by Clutterbuck, mentioned in the chapter. Additional material is to be found in M. G. Zey, *The mentor connection*, Dow-Jones Irwin, 1984

D. Hunt and C. Michael, 'Mentorship', in *Academy of Management Review*, Vol 8, No 3, 1983

K. Kram, 'Phases of the mentor relationship', *Academy of Management Journal*, Vol 6, No 4, December 1983

D. Meginson, 'Instructor, coach, mentor: three ways of helping for managers', *Management Education and Development*, Vol 19, Part 1, 1988

Chapter 8

D. Binsted and R. Stuart, 'Designing reality into management learning events', *Personnel Review*, Vol 8, No 3, 1979 gives the best conceptual analysis of this.

A useful integrative article is:

G. Prideaux and J. E. Ford, 'Management development: competencies, contracts, teams, and work based learning'. *Journal of Management Development*, Vol 7, No 1, 1988

Criticisms of business schools and particularly of MBA programmes have been more prolific than supportive articles. In the UK see

N. Foy, *The missing links*, Foundation for Management Education, 1978

and in the United States

J. N. Behrman and R. I. Levin, 'Are business schools doing their job?', *Harvard Business Review*, Jan/Feb 1984

The alternative UK view is put by

J. Forrester, *A study of the practical uses of the MBA*, BIM, 1984

Outdoor Training, the new attractive technique, is described by

J. Bank, *Outdoor development for managers*, Gower, 1985

There are two curate's egg books on management training:

A. Pepper, *Managing the training and development function*, Gower, 1984

This is good on the organization of training, but not on learning or on management development in total.

J. E. Jones and M. Woodcock, *Manual of management development*, Gower, 1985 also has good guidance on courses and does actually address the processes of learning.

Chapter 9

Many of the relevant books here have been mentioned in earlier chapters.

In addition to the books on bosses by Mumford and McCall mentioned earlier, an article by M. London, 'The boss's role in management development', *Journal of Management Development*, Vol 5, No 3, 1986 is worth reading for its specific cases.

An article by Garavan is also particularly helpful:

'Promoting natural learning activities within the organisation', *Journal of European Industrial Training*, Vol 11, No 7, 1987

The article by Roger Stuart, 'Maximising managers' day-to-day learning: framework for the practice of learning interventions', is, as often with him, both thought-provoking and practical (published in *Management development: advances in theory and practice*, edited by C. Cox and J. Beck, Wiley, 1984).

The work by Pepper mentioned above is the prime source of material on trainers and advisers here. From quite a different perspective, but dealing very much with the kind of activities in which developers and trainers may get involved, see

A. Huczynski, *Encyclopedia of management development methods*, Gower, 1983

See also R. Bennett, *Improving trainer effectiveness*, Gower, 1988

Chapter 10

The most stretching statement about women is:

J. Marshall, *Travellers in a male world*, Wiley, 1984

Another substantial contribution is:

C. Cooper and M. Davidson, *Women in management*, Heinemann, 1984

A useful collection of case studies is:

Women of the 80s, published by Manpower Services Commission, 1987

Ashton applies Hofstede's analysis of national culture to his then organization in:

'Cultural differences: implications for management development', *Management Education and Development*, Vol 15, Part 1, 1984

Other aspects are usefully described in:

J. W. Seddon, 'The Education and Development of Overseas Managers', *Management Education and Development*, Vol 16, Part 1, 1985

R. T. Pascale and A. G. Athos, *The art of Japanese management*, Penguin, 1982

T. Vineall, 'Creating a multinational management team', *Personnel Management*, October 1988

Multicultural management development, Special Issue of *Journal of Management Development*, Vol 6, No 3, 1987

Chapter 11

A number of the relevant articles and books are identified in the article by Mumford: 'Self development: missing elements'. *Industrial and Commercial Training*, Vol 18, No 3, 1986

Some useful directions for improvement in the self-development process are indicated in P. Honey and N. Povah 'Self development: overcoming the paradox'. *Industrial and Commercial Training*, Vol 18, No 4, 1986

On the learning process there is no major alternative to Kolb's book (*Experiential learning*). The only other major conceptual work is Patricia Cross, *Adults as learners*, Jossey Bass, 1981.

The whole field of 'learning to learn' was reviewed by Mumford in 'Learning to learn for managers: a literature review', *Management Bibliographies and Reviews*, Vol 12, No 2, 1986

See also John Morris on the learning spiral in the *Gower Handbook of Management Development*, 198

The articles by Stuart referenced in the chapter are very useful.

Ian Cunningham offers a different approach to that of the learning cycle or learning styles, he describes this as 'patterns'. This approach could be particularly helpful for those who do not favour the structured diagnostic instrument approach.

I. Cunningham, in *Beyond distance teaching: – towards open learning*, Open University Press, 1987

Although misleadingly titled, Bob Garrat's book *The learning organisation*, Gower 1987, contains some excellent work on directors, their thinking and learning processes. This should be read in association with:

E. H. Schein, *Organisational culture and leadership*, Jossey Bass, 1987

Some very exciting ideas about the use of colleagues in development are given in:

K. Kram and L. Isabella, 'Alternatives to mentoring', *Academy of Management Journal*, Vol 28, No 1, March 1985

All Chapters

The new Chapter 13 in this second edition discusses books or articles relevant to a number of points in previous chapters. Reference should therefore be made to that chapter when reviewing the material mentioned above.

There are two handbooks on management development. Reference has been made to a number of entries in the Gower publication which I edited. Particularly useful chapters supplementing the existing references are Tony Vineall on planning management development for Chapters 5 and 6, and Peter Bramley on evaluation for Chapter 8.

The other handbook is the *Management development and training handbook*, edited by B. Taylor and G. Lippitt, second edition, McGraw Hill, 1984. This useful collection of articles looks at some processes not covered in this book.

Finally, the IPM has produced a book *Continuous development* which illustrates its own interest in combining formal and informal learning, with a number of specific cases.

Rosemary Harrison's *Training and development*, IPM, 1988 is an excellent book. Although aimed at a wider population than managers, it gives helpful guidance on the design and review of learning experiences.

Mumford's Desert Island Books

The references I have made to books and articles so far have been to produce data, to create or support a case. In this last section I have attempted to provide some protection against a total domination of my own interests and ideas. As I worked on this book, and particularly as I produced the references in this last section, I thought that here was an opportunity for a final exercise. The book began by asking readers to describe a powerful learning experience. It ends by inviting them to carry out a similar exercise.

Which written or visual piece of material has been of most significance to you in considering, or working on, management development? (It may be a film, a case study, an article or a book.)

I have been most powerfully influenced by the written word. The following list is not, in fact, that of the books that have influenced me most, but those that I would choose to take to a desert island. The criteria for choice are that the book should offer me the prospect of continuing to learn from a rereading of it. This has eliminated some books which powerfully influenced me in the past, but which I feel I have sapped dry. Here is my choice.

John Kotter, *The general managers*, Free Press, 1982

Rosemary Stewart, *Choices for the manager*, McGraw Hill, 1982

David Kolb, *Experiential learning*, Prentice Hall, 1983

Charles Handy, *Understanding organizations*, Penguin, 1985

McCall *et al.*, *The lessons of experience*, Lexington, 1988

John Garbarro, 'When a new manager takes charge', *Harvard Business Review*, May 1985.

Peter Honey, *Improve your people skills*, IPM, 1988

A. Huczynski, *Encyclopedia of management development methods*, Gower, 1983

13   A Review of Recent Developments

This new chapter looks at the question of whether there have been new ideas or techniques for management development which have come forward since the first edition. The approach has been to take a number of themes, each of which contains elements which might be attached to several of the earlier chapters.

A PHILOSOPHY, SYSTEM OR MODEL FOR MANAGEMENT DEVELOPMENT

Chapters 1 and 2 present my view of what management development is about. Of two major subsequent books, Charles Margerison's *Making Management Development Work* (McGraw-Hill, 1991) presents views which have a great deal in common with the ideas expressed in this book. He is largely concerned with learning from and within real work. He has a particularly valuable chapter entitled 'What do managers want from management development?' In essence, the focus of his ideas is on defining and meeting the needs of the organization – a process covered in detail in Chapters 4 to 6 of this book.

An alternative focus which offers a substantially different view of what management development is about appears in Gordon McBeath's *Practical Management Development* (Blackwell, 1990). His focus is almost entirely on systems and structured organized processes – described as Type 3 in my model in Chapter 2. Although he presents no model of management development which could be compared with mine, his implicit beliefs about the nature of management development come over clearly. To him, it is about systems, structures and the completion of forms, a view which I would regard as representing a well-delivered version of *formal* management development.

Two other attempts to review the nature of management development should also be highlighted. John Storey has reviewed the literature in two articles 'Management Development: A literature review and implications for future research' (*Personnel Review*, Vol 18, No 6, 1989, and Vol 19, No 1, 1990). These two articles are required reading for anybody who wants to survey the whole field and needs some help in identifying the issues.

Stan Lees in 'Ten Faces of Management Development' (*Management Education and Development*, Vol 23, Part II, 1992) presents a quite different kind of review. He proposes 10 very different reasons why organizations support management development. His article will probably be of greater value than Storey's for many management development practitioners. They may find it odd, however, that Lees does not refer to Margerison, McBeath or indeed Mumford!

In fact, by far the largest attempt to redefine the nature of management development seems to me to be the movement towards a competency base. I add to my initial reference in Chapter 6 later in this chapter. At this point I want to state that the explicit beliefs of the national competency approach, and the implicit messages delivered through it, in at least one sense revise the purpose of management development. The national competency movement is directed at providing a management qualification. The view taken is that a competency approach is best geared not only to producing more effective managers, but that attaching a qualification represents the best strategy. As a result, the substantial money and energy devoted partly through the Department of Employment and partly through seconded members of industry imply, in my view, a substantially altered approach to what management development is for. While the proponents of the competency approach still argue in terms of increased reality and effectiveness, the actual effect of their work is to redefine management development in terms of what an individual can write and be examined on. If carried through, this philosophy would of course have a major impact on the management development work actually carried out.

DEVELOPING THE INDIVIDUAL

The competency approach through the Management Charter Initiative at national level (see Chapter 6) has burgeoned over the last three years. We now have statements for level I and II in terms of Personal Competences, standards and, crucially, methods of assessment. Earlier, I expressed doubts about the relevance or utility of national competencies, and I retain those doubts. The presumption that national standards can be defined and agreed in a way which is meaningful at an organizational, let alone an individual, level flies in the face of management research which shows the contingent, situational nature of management.

If we make the generous assumption that those responsible have actually read the research demonstrating this, we must ask why they have chosen to ignore it. One possibility would be that there is a continuing belief in the generic nature of management. A second reason seems more likely to have been the determining factor. This is the view that management is a profession; a profession has examinations or other processes for determining membership, and membership by qualification implies that each individual should satisfy general national standards. In the previous section, I argued that the consequence of this in philosophical terms is that management development becomes qualification–centred, despite its apparent adherence to meeting competency requirements. It will be a matter for each reader of this book to decide whether this philosophy and approach seem appropriate to the organization in which he or she works.

It is still much too early to say whether the impact of this philosophy and qualification–centred approach, when introduced into more than pilot organizations, will survive. The assessment process – the means by which it is decided whether an individual has or does not have competence – has already been removed from managers. It is conducted through assessment centres, which arguably means that the most important competence is the competence of writing about your competence. The most substantial gleam of light I can see in this whole process is the area of what was originally called Accrediting Prior Learning. Now described as Crediting Competence, this means that the assessment of a manager's competence is done through a portfolio describing actual experiences. The identification of the need for such a portfolio, and then of learning opportunities in order to be able to describe what you have achieved, seems wholly beneficial to me.

Unfortunately, one of the major potential results of the

Management Charter Initiative – the creation of networks of people and organizations interested in management development – has been much less the focus of attention. While large numbers of organizations accepted the Code of Practice, there seems as yet to be no written evidence that this has led to any change in management development – at any rate, people are not writing about it. Another idea which came out of discussion about the Management Charter Initiative, learning agreements between individuals and organizations, has had a more demonstrable impact. Clearly there is an association with the APL and Crediting Competence approach mentioned earlier. A most useful book on this is George Boak's *Developing Managerial Competences: The Management Learning Contract Approach* (Pitman, 1991). This is a very relevant extension of some of the ideas in Chapter 6.

Some of the more familiar ideas about self-development, though with the familiar and unfortunate failure to give enough attention to individual learning processes, are covered in Mike Pedler's collection *Self Development in Organisations* (McGraw-Hill, 1990).

Finally, the last three years seem to have continued the move towards some version of action learning in many organizations. Indeed, many business schools claim that this represents part of their programme – although on examination this seems to mean only that they now include projects, rather than changing at all the basic structure and philosophy of their courses. Mike Pedler is again the editor of a revised collection of articles *Action Learning in Practice* (2nd ed, McGraw-Hill, 1991). My own article 'Learning in Action' (*Personnel Management*, July 1991) gives a view of what we have learned about action learning over the last 20 years. It suggests that action learning should not be seen as an isolated technique, a particular way of getting managers to learn. It should be seen rather as a major vehicle for integrating different types and situations of learning so that the full power generated by a particular action learning experience is taken through to meet the often unobtained objective of continued learning after the programme. (See particularly Chapters 7 and 8 for other comments on action learning.)

MANAGERS AS HEROS

Although his managerial reputation has declined since the first edition of this book, I believe Lee Iacocca's book *Iacocca* (Bantam,

1986) is still the best in its genre as an explicit description of how senior managers learned.

John Harvey-Jones's first book, *Making It Happen* (Fontana, 1988), also presents some useful insights about development processes, and he is unusual amongst top executives in mentioning explicitly some off-the-job activities he has been through. My own conclusion about these books is increasingly that they are an interesting read, but are unlikely to form a useful part of organized management development. Perhaps we are growing weary with a succession of industrial leaders who sparkle for a time and then disappear. (Not, I hasten to add, a comment about John Harvey-Jones, who has remained very visible through his television programmes.) Perhaps we are finally coming to the conclusion that focusing development on the extraordinary characteristics of particular individuals is helpful neither to the organization nor to development processes.

The attempt to differentiate leaders and managers, described in Chapter 6, has continued with another book by W. Bennis *On Becoming a Leader* (Hutchinson Business Books, 1989). One of the earliest writers trying to establish this difference, Abraham Zaleznik, returned to the subject with *The Managerial Mystique: Restoring Leadership in Business* (Harper and Row, 1990). John Kotter, like Bennis, produced a second book on leadership *A Force for Change: How Leadership Differs from Management* (Free Press, 1990). As would be expected, Kotter's book is based on major research, Bennis's on extended case studies, and Zaleznik's on psychological theory. While there are useful insights in all three of these books, they are insights within a theory of differentiation which I find as unrealistic and as unhelpful as I did when writing the first edition of this book.

PEOPLE WHO HELP DEVELOPMENT

The increased attention to development on and through the job inevitably throws greater weight on managers themselves as developers of others. Surprisingly little is available on this, other than the books on coaching mentioned in Chapter 12, and the very welcome second edition of Clutterbuck's *Everyone Needs a Mentor* (IPM, 1991). My own article 'Helpers in Management Development' (*Executive Development*, Vol 5, No 2, 1992) extends some of the comments made in Chapter 9 of this book. A major extension of these ideas and practices will be available in *Managers as Developers*

(Gower, 1993). A number of the issues mentioned already really come together under this heading, in the sense that all the work-based learning, all the facilitation of learners on the job, the processes of coaching, mentoring and mutual problem solving have essentially to be carried out by line managers, however much professional developers may previously have helped on what should be done. I would expect in the next edition of this book to be able to refer to a much wider range of resources and techniques.

THE LEARNING ORGANIZATION

Some of the early literature on the learning organization has been referred to in Chapter 11. Since that time there have been two major books extending our understanding of what might be involved: *The Learning Company* by M. Pedler, J. Burgoyne and T. Boydell (McGraw-Hill, 1991) and *The Fifth Discipline* by P. Senge (Century, 1990). As an alternative to the definition of learning organizations offered by Pedler and his colleagues (see pages 207–8), we now can cite Senge's:

> Organizations where people continually expand their capacity to create the results they truly desire, where new and expansive patterns of thinking are nurtured, where collective aspiration is set free, and where people are continually learning how to learn together.

Senge is a great devotee of Systems Thinking, and also influenced by the work of Chris Argyris. Pedler and his colleagues have built on their marvellously original and helpful contributions on self-development, and their views on what (I think rather perversely) they call the learning company are imbued by issues of ethics, quality and personal growth. The problem with both books is that they take such a broad view of the circumstances in which an organization does or needs to learn that the idea of learning becomes lost in a total vision of what a good organization might be like. Most trainers and management developers would be unlikely to be able to get to grips with the kind of issues which these books raise as being fundamental. So high level are their concerns that, for example, Senge avoids any consideration of learning skills in his list of seven Learning Disabilities.

The growing attractiveness of the concept of the learning organization is currently making it one of the front runners for the management development mode of the 1990s. However, there are clearly major problems of interpretation in what is meant to be covered. As yet there is a significant absence of clear association with useful learning practices developed through organizational rather than individual or group themes. In terms of practical help on how to achieve the learning organization, very little is available.

Indeed, what is available seems to me to be pretty much old wine put into new bottles. I do not assert this as a criticism of the books by Pedler and Senge. I am referring to the subsequently published articles by a number of authors who are now giving the title organizational learning to a variety of activities which would three or four years ago have been described as action learning, organization development or quality circles. From the management development perspective it seems absolutely necessary for us not to adopt too readily the latest cliché – a recipe for confusing ourselves about what we are attempting.

While management development advisers can usefully think in terms of a learning organization, they should not think first of courses and formal systems of development. Equally, it is perhaps not very helpful for most of us to ascend into the higher realms of total organizational quality. The definition of the learning organization offered by myself and Peter Honey as an appropriate starting point to help managers avoid these errors is:

THE LEARNING ORGANIZATION
Creating an Environment
Where the behaviours and practices involved in
Continuous Development are actively encouraged

This captures most of the issues raised in the checklist on pages 13 and 14 of Chapter 1.

Index